Scammell

First published in 1997 by Roundoak Publishing
The Old Dairy, Perry Farm, East Nynehead,
Wellington, Somerset, England TA21 0DA

Copyright 1997 Roundoak Publishing & Nick Georgano

ISBN 1 871565 26 X

Reprographics: Character Graphics, Taunton

Printed in England by
The Amadeus Press, Huddersfield

Jacket cover and this page:
A.L.E. bought two Mk 2 Contractors from Econofreight and after returning them to their original red paint scheme they were shipped to Abu Dhabi where they continue to prosper. They are seen here at work in 1992 hauling a refinery column of 435 tons on a combination of Goldhofer and Scheuerle trailers. They were photographed by Roger Colcombe, driver of the lead vehicle.

Scammell
The Load Movers
from Watford

Nick Georgano

Contents

KD 5096, numbered 61 in the M.R.S. Ltd. fleet, is pictured here in the late 1930s near the village of Hilton, in the then county of Huntingdonshire, conveying south a casting manufactured by John Brown of Sheffield. Raised up on cross-laid bulks of timber – to clear the drop-frame trailer's rear four-in-line wheelset – the 16ft. wide load requires the crew's full attention as it crosses the bridge. Note the opened engine side panel evidence that the venerable Scammell's petrol engine was having to work hard on the summer's day hauling the oversized load.

Introduction

Scammell fever struck me early. I cannot have been more than six years old when a column of fairground vehicles passed our front gate in Middlesex, shortly before World War 2. Even the steam showman's engines with their twisted brass cab standards did not have as much appeal as the hard-working chain driven Scammell tractors. At about the same time photographs of the 100-tonner, cut from The Commercial Motor, took pride of place in my scrapbook. A few years later I compiled a fanciful catalogue for a variety of vehicles based on the Mechanical Horse including long-wheelbase five wheelers for goods and passenger work.

The variety and ingenuity of Scammell designs are a fascination for any transport enthusiast. The turntable with separate springing to carry the weight of the trailer, albeit derived from an American design, was an essential part of Europe's first quantity-produced articulated six wheeler, while Oliver North's ingenious double axle drive on the Pioneer allowed remarkable cross-country performance. At the other end of the scale, the Mechanical Horse played an essential role in moving local delivery work from the horse to motor transport.

Throughout their history, Scammell's role was not just making vehicles but providing solutions for transport problems. They were also one of the first British firms to take the export market seriously, and to make purpose built trucks for desert and other off-road work. Their reward was a world-wide market, with customers in the Middle East, India, Africa, Latin America, Australia and Russia. The Armed Forces, too, were keen Scammell customers, from the Pioneer tank transporters of the 1930s to their successor of fifty years later, the Commander whose descendants are still made by Unipower.

I hope that this book, containing as it does much information and photographs not seen in previous Scammell histories, will provide a fitting tribute to the men of Tolpits Lane who made them, and the drivers all over the world who have spent so much of their working lives at the wheel of Scammell lorries.

Nick Georgano
Guernsey
January 1997

Below: Pickford's Scammell Highwayman M 2076, one of a batch of ballasted tractors that went into service with the company in 1958, parked up with its lengthy load of a petrol distillation column on a pair of Crane bogies on a cold January morning in 1967 at Butterbusk, near Doncaster. These tractors were capable of hauling loads of 55 tons or more.

Acknowledgements

A book like this is inevitably a joint effort, in that so much information comes from a variety of sources. First, I would like to thank Arthur Ingram, who has provided the majority of the photographs from his magnificent collection, and has also give much helpful advice with captioning. Others who have helped with photographs and information include Alan Baker, Nick Baldwin, Bryan Blow, Kevin Cobb, Peter Connock, Adrian Cypher, Peter Davies, Les Freathy, Terry Gander, Alan Godfree, Jean-Jacques Horb, Bill Ladbrooke, David Lee, Jack London, Keith Nicholl, R.D. Palmer, Martin Phippard, David Stretton, Richard Tew, Bart Vanderveen, The Scammell Register and The Tank Museum, Bovington.

Two former Scammell employees who have given most generously of their time to answer a barrage of questions are Mick Green, who joined the sales staff in 1948 and retired as export sales manager in 1983, and Edward Riddle who was Chief Designer from 1967 to 1978, and who was a part-time consulting engineer for both Scammell and Unipower up to 1985. Also another ex-Scammell man who wishes to remain anonymous.

The staff at Unipower have been very helpful on recent history, in particular, Peter Rotheroe, Chairman, Roger Holmes, General Sales Manager and Glyn Rees, Vehicle Sales Manager.

Others who have given invaluable help in many ways include Ray Coleman (Lantern Group), Bob Gwilliam, Ferdy Hediger, Sydney and Brian Harrison (S. Harrison & Sons Ltd), Andre Horb, Jack Kimp, Secretary of the Scammell Register, Frank Bone and Geoff Morant.

Thanks also go to Pamela and Fred Jackson for their help in the genealogical research of the Scammell family, to Keith Moore, Senior Librarian/Archivist, Institution of Mechanical Engineers and finally Annice Collett and Paul Beard of the National Motor Museum Library, who spent hours photostatting magazines and catalogues for me.

Below: Interior of Fashion Street workshops with Foden steam wagons, circa 1914.

CHAPTER ONE

From Handcarts to Hundred Tonners

Though complete trucks did not appear until after the First World War, the Scammell name has an ancestry older than any other British vehicle builder. The trucks were made by an offshoot of G. Scammell & Nephew, body-builders and repairers of steam and petrol vehicles, whose history dated back, so the company claimed, to 1837, the year that the eighteen-year old Victoria came to the throne.

Their earliest products were simple two-wheeled handcarts which could be easily manoeuvred around the narrow streets of Spitalfields, in London's East End, where the company was founded. The premises were in Fashion Street, which ran between Bethnal Green Road and Mile End Road, right in the heart of a bustling area of small industries, clothiers, furriers, toolmakers, and so on. By the end of the nineteenth century it would have a large population of immigrants from Eastern Europe, though these were probably not so evident fifty years earlier.

Scammells soon turned to horse-drawn vehicles, mostly for commercial work, though a number of handsome carriages were made as well. As the company history claimed a foundation date of 1837, it is possible that George Scammell (1817-1874) was already an employee, though the London Trades Directory for 1837 cites the proprietor of the business at 46 Fashion Street as S.Hagger, wheelwright. By 1851 George was listed as proprietor, and twenty years later the name George Scammell & Nephew had been adopted. The nephew was Alfred Thomas

Scammell (1850-1921), the son of George's brother Thomas who was a miller at Stalbridge, Dorset.

They were a West Country family, George being born at Donhead St. Mary, Wiltshire. Two other brothers were also millers, William at Cann, Dorset, and John at Liphook, Hampshire. It was during the regime of Alfred Thomas that Scammells began to take on repair work for steam and motor vehicles in the early Edwardian period. By 1913 they were the leading agent for Foden steam wagons in the London area, and were also selling Commer petrol vehicles.

They had a busy workshop for the repair of Fodens, and by 1913 owned several properties in Fashion Street. In that year they expanded further by bringing into use a large building that they owned but which had been let to a tailoring firm. They now occupied so much of Fashion Street that 'The World's Carriers' magazine suggested that

Foden steam wagons under repair at Fashion Street, circa 1914.

An advertisement for G. Scammell & Nephew showing one of their horse-drawn vans, though steam wagon wheels and bodies were also listed.

the name might quite reasonably be changed to Scammell Street. Interestingly, 'The World's Carriers' report, carried in their September 15th 1914 issue, mentioned a rumour that the company had found it necessary to purchase land outside London for the erection of further workshops. It has always been thought that the move to Watford was occasioned by the arrival of the articulated lorry, but this rumour, if true, anticipated the lorry by six years.

Perhaps the war put paid to the expansion plans, though G. Scammell & Nephew were very busy providing Foden steam wagons to the Army Service Corps. Commandeered wagons from all over the country were sent to the Scammell works to be overhauled and fitted out as workshop and breakdown vehicles. By the end of the war

A Foden overtype steam wagon of the type provided for the Army by G. Scammell & Nephew. By 1918 more than 800 were in service, with general cargo and tipper bodies. This is a disinfector, used for removing vermin from soldiers' clothing. Steam was less popular than petrol for army vehicles, as supplies of coal and water had to be carried up to the front, and the plumes of smoke and steam revealed the vehicle's presence to the enemy.

more than 800 Fodens were in service with the British Army, and a high proportion of these must have passed through the Spitalfields workshops. In 1925 it was reported that Fashion Street could handle sixty to seventy heavy vehicles at a time, and employed 180 men. They continued to repair and sell Foden steamers, Commers and other makes up to the 1930s, and had a flourishing business stripping and reconditioning vehicles for a second lease of life. Another department carried on with body building. This continued after the Second World War, examples of their work being a mobile shop on a Morrison Electricar chassis in 1948, and furniture vans on Commers in the 1950s. The Fashion Street premises were sold in 1965, after Scammell & Nephew were taken over by the York Trailer Group.

It is not generally known that G. Scammell & Nephew tried to become makers of complete vehicles, in a venture quite separate from Scammell Lorries of Watford. In 1933 they built a forward control low-loading five-tonner powered by a 45 bhp Meadows 4EL four-cylinder engine. It

ran on small 27 x 6 inch tyres, and was a competitor for similar low-loaders built by Easyloader and Shelvoke & Drewry. The first was supplied to the Steel Barrel Company of Uxbridge, who made many of the frameless tankers for Scammell, and eventually merged with G. Scammell & Nephew. Possibly there was only the one; certainly it never became a production vehicle.

'The Knox Tractor'

The idea of building an articulated six-wheeler came from Alfred Thomas Scammell's son, Alfred George (1878-1941), who finished the war as a Lieutenant Colonel with a DSO. The concept of a single-axle semi trailer whose front end was attached to a tractor by means of a turntable was almost as old as the commercial vehicle. Thornycroft had built one in 1898, but had not exploited the idea, and a few had been made in America, by White of Cleveland, Ohio, among others. However the real ancestor of the Scammell was the tractor design by Charles H. Martin (1868-1953) of York, Pennsylvania. His design, which became a cornerstone of the Scammell layout, incorporated separate springing for the turntable which rested on the rear wheels of the tractor. This was by heavy semi-elliptic springs, while the weight of the tractor was carried on lighter underslung cantilever springs. The load on these remained constant regardless of the load carried by the semi-trailer.

Known as the Martin Rocking Fifth Wheel, the principle was put into production by the Knox Motors Company of Springfield, Massachusetts. The first Knox-Martin tractors had a single front wheel with a steering lock of nearly 90°, which enabled the tractor to turn in its own length. Even with semi-trailer its turning circle was remarkably small. The engine was a 40 hp four-cylinder ohv unit with detachable head, of 6110 cc, driving through a separate three-speed gearbox and double chains from a countershaft. Introduced as the Model 31 in 1909, the three-wheel tractor was very popular in America, where it was used as a motive unit for fire engines, as well as for brewery and general haulage work. It was tested by the US Army, but on rough ground three separate wheel tracks were a disadvantage, and this led to the four-wheeled tractor known as the Model 35.

Introduced in 1915, the Model 35 had a similar engine to the Model 31, enlarged to 7075 cc, and with pair-cast, in place of separate, cylinders. A most unusual feature was hydraulic operation of the rear-wheel brakes. As with many vehicles at this time, the wheel brakes were operated by a lever rather than a pedal, and the large lever performed the action of a pump handle. It was possible to lock the wheels, even when fully loaded and descending a hill, by three or four strokes of the lever. The most extreme test of this involved a hill of 1 in 10 and a special load of 70 tons. The Knox remained in that position for four days without a loss of braking pressure. The normal loading for the Model 35 was 10 tons, though in French Army service they often carried tanks weighing 13.5 tons.

The French Army took 121 Knox tractors, the British far fewer, only six tractors and nine trailers. After the Armistice demobbed examples quickly came into the hands of civilian hauliers. One who was particularly impressed by the Knox was E.W. Rudd, whose company, based at Bow Common Lane, London E.3, had been active in meat transport since the 1890s. At least one Knox Model 35 had been seen in England as early as 1915, when it received a favourable review in 'The Commercial Motor', including mention of the braking test referred to. Perhaps Rudd inspected this example, or perhaps he saw, or heard of a military version. Anyway, he quickly became sole agent for Knox tractors for Britain and the Empire, with the exception of Canada. By December 1922, when 'Motor Transport' reviewed his meat transport operations, he had thirty Knoxes, six Scammells, and eighteen steamers, twelve Fodens and six Garretts, as well as some smaller Commer and Dennis lorries. He also sold a number of Knox tractors to Pickfords.

'The Scammell Six-Wheeled Tractor-Lorry'

This cumbersome description was used by journalists to describe the vehicle which took shape in the Fashion Street works during 1919. It was certainly a new concept for the British industry, described by 'The World's Carriers' as 'a new departure in motor transport'. How much Alfred Scammell was influenced by the Knox will never be known, but there were some striking similarities. The turntable with separate springing to carry the weight of the trailer was very similar in principle, though the springs of the tractor chassis were semi-elliptic in place of the Knox's rather frail-looking cantilevers. The engine had identical bore and stroke, and the same valve layout, detachable heads and pair-casting of cylinders. The separate three-speed gearbox and double chain drive were the same, though these were common features of many heavy vehicles. The Knox's ingenious hydraulic brakes were not adopted by Scammell, which had a footbrake operating on the transmission between the gearbox and the differential, and handbrakes on the rear wheels of the tractor and on the trailer.

Before going ahead with the lorry, Scammell had to ensure that their design would be legal on British roads. The law restricted a tractor towing a trailer to 5 mph, but this limit was drawn up with traction engines in mind. The Scammell could claim to be a single unit, thus legal up to 12 mph so long as no axle carried more than six tons. As the total weight of tractor and trailer with a platform body was under five tons, this allowed a payload of seven tons. '7½ Tons at 3 Ton Cost and Speed' ran the lettering on the side of the demonstration lorry, and if the operators was prepared to put up with a 5 mph restriction, the Scammell could be had with a full trailer behind, with a payload of a further six tons. It does not seem however, that any were delivered in this form; both performance and manoeuvrability, good selling points for the tractor/trailer unit, would have been greatly reduced with an extra trailer.

Top: A Knox Model 35 tractor with trailer in the jack-knife position, showing its small turning circle. The trailer may well be a modified horse-drawn wagon. The US Army used one of these and one four-wheeled full trailer behind three- and four-wheeled Knoxes. The number A-FMA-3 is a trade plate.

Middle: A Knox Model 35 in Pickfords livery, photographed on the corner of Russell Street, Plaistow, east London, in 1920. Behind it are a Model TT Ford, and a Tilling-Stevens.

Bottom: In contrast to the Pickfords Knox, with military type open cab, this one operated by E.W. Rudd has a windscreen and panel behind the cab, also an oversize radiator. In addition to the Model 35, Knox made a tractor with ballast body for full trailers, called the Model 36.

An interesting photo showing the six wheeler with additional six ton trailer. This would have reduced its legal speed from 12 to 5 mph, and so far as is known none were delivered in this form. The photo, minus the trailer, was used to illustrate Motor Traction's road test published in June 1920.

'Move to Watford'

The Scammell six wheeler was tested by the commercial vehicle press in June 1920, when the company was already described as 'Messrs Scammell & Nephew of Spitalfields and Watford.' This contradicts claims sometimes made that the move to Watford was only a result of demand generated by the make's appearance at the 1921 Olympia Show. Although construction of the prototype was only a side-line in the Fashion Street works, Alfred Scammell must have realised that if his idea took off, new premises would have to be found, and it is likely that the factory at Tolpits Lane, Watford, seventeen miles north west of London, was taking shape at the same time as the few pioneer lorries, probably not more than ten, were being built at Spitalfields. In 1919-21 Scammell also had a small premises at Radlett Road, Watford, on the site of Newman's Nursery, but it is not known if any vehicle building was carried out there.

As there was no Commercial Motor Show in 1920, the Scammell was displayed to the public that summer by

Chassis view of an early tractor showing the separate gearbox, chain drive and turntable for the trailer. The rear of the heavy semi-elliptic spring can just be seen below the turntable. The double brake levers, for tractor and trailer, are visible on the off side.

appearances at big manufacturing towns and at the Royal Agricultural Show at Darlington. The lone demonstrator was driven by sales manager R.H. Johnson and his assistant G.A. Wadham, and it was said that they and the lorry were very hard worked during the summer of 1920. 'Motor Traction' observed that '...the Scammell attracted considerable attention in Coventry, where the inhabitants are so accustomed to seeing every type of motor vehicle, from the motor scooter upward, that it requires something very much out of the ordinary to make a Coventry man look twice - which the Scammell did.'

Scammell's first motor show appearance was at Olympia in November 1921, when they exhibited a 2000 gallon oil tanker for Shell Mex and a furniture van for Maples, 'reputed to be the largest industrial vehicle ever made', said 'The Commercial Motor'. They also showed an American-built Towmotor industrial tractor, for which G. Scammell & Nephew were agents. By then the six-wheelers were already in service with a variety of users, including well-known hauliers such as Fairclough, Fisher Renwick and E.W. Rudd, brewers Tamplin of Brighton, Strong of Romsey and Friary of Guildford, and oil companies Shell-Mex and Anglo Persian. When 'The World's Carriers' visited Watford in the autumn of 1921 they found the works 'comparatively more busy than the majority of factories we have visited for some time. We do not mean to say that they are booked up for twelve months ahead.....but having regard to all things, they are finding a steady and growing demand for this remarkable vehicle.'

It was soon found that the Scammell could carry loads of up to 10 tons at speeds well above the legal 12 mph, and even with an additional five-ton trailer, 12 mph was possible, though not legal in the UK. Quite a number were going for export by the end of 1921. The first export sale went to the Gold Coast (now Ghana) and was believed to have remained in service for more than forty years.

Production was well under way by 1922, the year in which Scammell Lorries Ltd was formed as a separate

Phone :
6,50 AVENUE.
(4 lines).

Scammell Six Wheeler

Telegrams :
"SCAMWHEEL,
ALD., LONDON."

MEX FUEL OIL
SHELL MEX LTD KINGSWAY

MEX FUEL OIL

MEX FUEL OIL

The Scammell—Tank Wagon.

Capacity	2,200 gallons	any trailer
Petrol Consumption	5/6 M.P.G.	with trailer, 4/5 M.P.G.
Oil Consumption	400 M.P.G.	300 M.P.G.
Mean Speed	12 M.P.H.	10 M.P.H.

Tank is of Welded Steel Plate, suitably baffled and stayed, exhaust is carried through the tank to heat contents. Pumping by independent set operated by Marine Motor, coupled to Feuerheerd Pump, capacity 5,000 gallons per hour at 60° F. at 70ft. head, empties or fills tank in 20 minutes. Similar Tanks are supplied riveted and of circular, or oval section. Twenty machines, as illustrated, are in use by Shell-Mex Ltd.

Left: Extract from the 1922 catalogue, showing the tanker for Shell-Mex which was on the Scammell stand at the 1922 Olympia Show. By 1922 twenty had been supplied to Shell. The 2200 gallon tank was built by Fraser & Fraser of Bromley-by-Bow, London E.3. The tanker carried crude oil, not petrol, and to keep this in a reasonably fluid state for easy pumping, the exhaust was carried through the tank. At the rear a Kelvin 7 hp marine-type 2-cylinder engine drove a pump to fill or empty the tank.

long time; their attachments were called carriers, probably to distinguish them from the two-axle full trailers which were still restricted to 5 mph. The towing vehicles were called motive units rather than tractors, this term being reserved for vehicles operating with drawbar trailers.

The 7-litre engine changed little, though output grew to more than 85 bhp. In 1925 Scammell made about 35 marine versions, with bronze castings to allow for sea water cooling. They were intended for pinnaces of the former German fleet, most of which had been scuppered at Scapa Flow. Scammell also made marine engines in World War 2, but these were mechanical horse units.

A very important development of 1924 was the frameless tanker. Earlier tankers such as the Shell-Mex trailer used tank bodies mounted on conventional channel section frames, but the frameless design was just that. The tank formed its own frame, and was supported by a pair of double solid tyres whose semi-elliptic springs were attached to the tank by brackets riveted to stiffening plates, which were in turn riveted to the tank. Elimination of the chassis frame meant a saving of about 15 cwt (762kg), which could go towards additional load capacity without exceeding the axle weight limit. The first frameless tanker was supplied to Shell-Mex in June 1924, with three more following soon afterwards. The frameless tanker, which became a Scammell speciality, was later used for other liquids, including beer, milk, molasses, industrial acids and also powders and gases. By 1930 about 200 were in service.

The six wheeler with its various trailers was the sole product of the Watford works until 1927 when it was joined by the Pioneer rigid six wheeler, which will be described in a later chapter. The end of the decade saw two new models, a rigid four for 6 ton loads, later uprated to an 8 tonner, and the remarkable 100 tonner which deserves a chapter to itself. Production in the 1920s was not large; chassis numbering began at 700 in 1922, and had only reached 1563 by August 1930; giving a total of 863 in eight seasons.

company, with factory operations entirely at Watford and offices in Holborn, London. The drawing office was at Holborn from 1924 to 1936. The factory location was to remain the same until the end of production in 1988. For the rest of the 1920s the six-wheeler story was one of gradual evolution and extension of the range, rather than any dramatic change. The original open cab with canvas top and sometimes no windscreen was joined by one with a fixed roof and screen, though no sidescreens, during 1922. Also in 1922 came a new type of trailer, the swan-necked drop frame cable carrier, originally for the General Post Office, though later used for a variety of jobs including carrying boilers and excavators. Load capacity was increased to 12 tons by using four wheels abreast on the trailer, this being known as the eight wheeler. By 1928 dropframe trailers with a 25 ton capacity were being used. Incidentally, Scammell did not use the word trailer for a

Above: Another tanker with a more unusual load; an awful lot of shoes could be polished with the contents, if they were actual boot polish, but in fact the tank is carrying oil used in the manufacture of the polish.

Below: A straight-framed trailer carrying a steel girder considerably longer than the whole vehicle, for the Battersea-based structural steel fabricators and engineers, A.D. Dawnay Ltd.

Left: Known as the cable trolley, this was the first drop frame low-loader made by Scammell. This example was operated by the Post Office Stores department, but similar ones were bought by Fisher Renwick. Using the hand operated winch at the front of the trailer, two men could load an 8-ton cable drum in a few minutes. The load area behind the crank in the frame was 12 feet long, but could be made longer to suit any purpose, said the catalogue. Three models were offered, to carry loads of 10, 12 or 15 tons.

Below: A later drop frame trailer, dating from c.1928, heads a line up of E.W.Rudd Scammells carrying transformers made by Hackbridge of Walton-on-Thames. The photograph shows eight of a total order of 25 18,750 KVA transformers which were destined for Canada. The motive units further back are on pneumatic tyres, which dates the photograph to the early 1930s.

Below left: Friary was one of several brewers to take up the Scammell six wheeler. The curved front to the box van was a Scammell speciality, and allowed for a greater angle of turn without the van fouling the back of the cab. Note the acetylene headlamps and oil sidelamps.

Below right: In contrast to the Friary vehicle, this unit for Drums Limited of Grays, Essex has electric lighting for both head and sidelamps. It has an exceptionally large dropframe pantechnicon body. Capacities were as high as 1600 cubic feet; anything smaller than 1100 cubic feet was built on a straight frame.

Left and below: Carrying capacity was increased to 12 tons by the employment of four wheels abreast on the trailer. There were separate axles for each pair of wheels, each axle having its own semi-elliptic leaf spring. There are considerable differences between the mounting of the axle to the frame in these two photos. The substantial bars linking the brackets are absent in the later vehicle below.

Opposite top: This eight wheeler is described in the maker's caption as a 17 tonner, presumably referring to the gross weight. The well-laden carrier is being loaded with barrels of South African apples for delivery to Covent Garden.

Opposite below: A further refinement of the twin axle layout came in 1928, when the axles could be removed and the rear of the trailer dropped to the ground to facilitate the loading of heavy machinery. The trailer floor then formed a ramp which could be bridged by a baulk of timber. It was claimed that the axles could be detached and rolled away in less than fifteen minutes. Capacity of this low-loader was 25 tons, and the principle was used for many years. The photo shows a 1939 version, by which time pneumatic tyres were used all round. The axles have been detached, but the ramp has yet to be completed.

Above: Another low-loading trailer with detachable rear axles, carrying a large works or dockyard oil-fired boiler. The trailer is by Taskers of Andover, and the registration number DTR 704 dates from early 1944. The tractor, operated by the Docks Haulage Co of Bitterne, Southampton, is probably several years older than the trailer.

Below left and below: The frameless tanker was one of Scammell's most important contributions to lorry design, saving about 15 cwt (762 kg) in trailer weight. As with the original tanker of 1921, Scammell's first customer for the frameless design was Shell. These photos show the 3000 gallon tanker before being lettered in Shell-Mex livery. Ahead of the radiator is an engine-driven three-cylinder air compressor used for forcing the contents of the tank through an outlet valve at the back. This was clearly a simpler method than the separate 2-cylinder compressor motor used in the 1921 tanker. Another improvement, seen on all frameless tankers, was that the tank was inclined slightly to the rear, to facilitate emptying.

Above: This view of a frameless beer tanker shows the cork insulation over glass lining. The cork would be covered by aluminium panelling. Frameless tankers were made by Scammell themselves, and also by the Steel Barrel Company of Uxbridge, which later merged with G. Scammell & Nephew.

Above: As with other trailers, frameless tankers could have conventional paired wheels or, as here, four in line on twin axles. Note the handle for the outlet valve, to which a flexible discharge pipe could be connected.

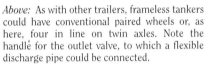

Left and below: Later examples of frameless tankers, the first, dating from 1930 with pneumatic tyres on the front wheels, the second, from 1932, with pneumatics all round. Garton, Sons & Co Ltd, makers of syrup and sugar, later became Manbre, Garton, who were Scammell customers up to the 1960s.

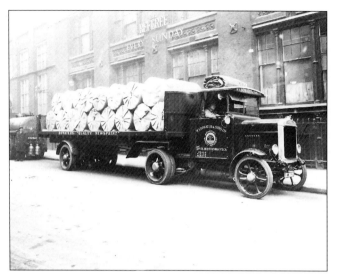

Left: This mid-twenties tractor with straight platform trailer is carrying paper from the well-known manufacturers, Bowater & Sons to Fleet Street newspapers. On the left are the premises of The Morning Post, which merged with The Daily Telegraph in 1937, and behind the lorry is located The Referee, a Sunday paper.

Middle: Operated by the Newcastle-on-Tyne Electric Supply Co Ltd, this trailer is fitted out as a mobile workshop for the standardisation of frequency which they were carrying out at factory sites, collieries, etc. Power for lighting the shop and driving the machines was supplied by a Parsons H4S engine with a 15 kilowatt generator. Machine tool equipment included grinders, a surfacing and screw cutting lathe and drilling machine. Note the Pelham Cranes with block and tackle at the centre and end of the trailer.

Bottom: Scammells had a thriving export market from their first year of production. This vehicle for the Venezuela Oil Company must date from around 1930, judging from its pneumatic tyres. Home market models of this date would no longer have had a canvas-top cab, but presumably the Venezuelan weather made a fixed roof unnecessary.

Above: In 1931 Scammell introduced their first eight wheeler with two pairs of axles arranged conventionally instead of two shorter rocking axles. It was rated for 14 tons, but could easily carry 17 tons. The single rear wheels were mounted on inverted semi-elliptic springs which were pivoted beneath substantial brackets welded to a cross member bolted to the frame. By comparison with the photo on page 14, the frame has changed little, though it now has one fewer cross member. The tyres were Goodyear low-pressure pneumatics, 9 x 20 inches on the front axle, 13.5 x 20 inches on the driving and trailer axles.

Below: This articulated eight-wheeler of about 1933 has a longer bonnet, indicating the presence of a six-cylinder diesel engine instead of Scammell's petrol four. Diesels, mainly by Dorman-Ricardo or Gardner, were used from 1931 onwards. Early examples had a very limited speed range, from around 800 to 1200 rpm, as they had been designed as stationary industrial engines. Purpose-designed diesels such as the Gardner LW series, came in from 1933 onwards. Coalville, Leicester-based hauliers Hutchby & Collumbell undertook work or contract for the nearby brick and tile manufacturers who continue to this day as Ibstock Johnsen plc.

Above: The carrying capacity of low-loaders rose steadily from the 12 tonners of 1922. The first trailers with detachable rear axles were rated for 25 tons, and in 1930 came a 40 tonner, still using the 7-litre 4-cylinder petrol engine. This is a 45 tonner, with diesel engine and pneumatic tyres on the front wheels. The illustration appeared in the catalogue as late as 1949, but the vehicle probably dates from the late 1930s.

Below: A mid 1930s petrol-engined articulated eight wheeler with shaft drive. This was introduced in 1933, though chains were available for some time longer. The new cab with sloping windscreen came in the mid 30s, though vertical screens were made at the same time.

Above: The 7-litre Scammell petrol engine was a very long-lived unit, being made in the same basic form from 1920 to 1940. In the original model, output was given as 47 bhp at 1000 rpm, though no accurate bench tests seem to have been made. Possibly it was nearer 60 bhp, and by 1931 quoted output was given as 85 bhp at 1800 rpm. Work was slack in the early 1930s, and to fill in time Frank Goodwin polished the ports of an engine. As a result it gave 92 bhp on test, but it was sent back to Goodwin to have the ports roughened up. "When we want an engine to give 92 bhp, we will make one" said management. Frank Goodwin was one of the few employees to exceed fifty years with the company, from joining at 14 in 1925 to retirement in 1976. This engine dates from about 1930; clearly visible is the Hobson atomiser manifold above the Claudel-Hobson carburetter. An electric starter was optional from 1934.

CHAPTER TWO

The Hundred Tonner

During 1929 a remarkable vehicle was taking shape at the Watford works, which was to extend the carrying capacity of a motor lorry beyond anything that had been thought of before. Up to that time, the heaviest indivisible load carried on a semi trailer was about 25 tons; anything larger went on one or more full trailers pulled by traction engines. These trailers had cast iron wheels, and open ended straight axles devoid of bearings. Several such trailers, built around the turn of the century, had been used by Marstons Road Services, whose head, Mr. E.C. Marston, worked closely with Scammell over the design of the 100 tonner, and took delivery of the first to be made. Marstons, which had become M.R.S. Ltd by 1929, were no strangers to Scammells, using several of the six wheelers which they converted to pneumatic tyres in 1932.

The 100 tonner had a different frame from the normal Scammells, being built up with riveted steel plates into a box frame, with apertures for the installation of engine, transmission and turntable. The engine was the standard 7-litre petrol unit, tuned to give 86 bhp. The gearbox was the standard four-speeder as well, but reduction gears at the ends of the countershaft gave eight forward speeds with a remarkable reduction of 196:1 in bottom gear. It was only with this low gearing that an 86 bhp engine could cope

with loads four times as high as those carried by smaller Scammells. Even so, more power was needed, and after a few years the petrol engine gave way to a Gardner 6LW developing 102 bhp. The biggest change came in fuel consumption, from 0.75 to 4.2 mpg. There were four driving wheels in a row on oscillating axles similar to the trailers on earlier Scammells, each wheel having paired solid tyres and its own chain drive from the countershaft.

The trailer, or carrier as Scammell still called it, had a massive swan neck linking it with the turntable, and either four or eight wheels at the rear. The first was for loads up to 65 tons, while all eight wheels were needed to support 100 tons. In fact during its lifetime the '100 tonner' carried loads as high as 165 tons. With a 100 ton load, the total axle loading was 120 tons. Between the swan neck and the rear bogies was the load carrying bed, a simple girder frame which could be made in two lengths. Relatively expendable, it was in one instance left behind to act as the base for stone crushing machinery which had been delivered to Cornwall. In another case it was sent overseas as a pallet for a turbo generator.

With the longest carrier, the 100 tonner was more than seventy feet long, and it was necessary to have a steersman at the rear. The bogies were steered by a large vertical wheel, and the steersman was also responsible for braking

The first 100 tonner, subsequently registered KD 9168 but here on trade plates, on demonstration to the press in November 1929. Note the external steering column; without power assistance, steering must have required very strong muscles. Load on the double cranked front axle was 8 tons, and lock to lock steering took seven turns of the wheel.

of the bogies. To communicate with the driver he had a telephone system operated from a little cabin, though if the load was very long the cabin had to be discarded and the steersman resorted to a whistle. Frequently the crew had to operate in extremely confined spaces; when transporting a 56 foot RAF launch from Harland & Woolf's yard at Bootle, the offside hubcap of the tractor brushed a wall, while the nearside of the boat's hull was less than the thickness of a pencil from the doorpost.

The M.R.S. 100 tonner, registered KD 9168, was joined by a similar vehicle delivered to H.E. Whey Ltd of Dartford, Kent, in February 1930. It was acquired by Pickfords in 1934, when it was registered BLH 21; its previous registration is not known. Both ended up with Pickfords, as KD 9168 was sold to Edward Box Ltd of Liverpool in about 1937 and passed on to Pickfords in 1949. They continued their heavy haulage careers well into the postwar period, being last taxed in December 1953. Taxation and licencing presented regular problems for operators, as no one could decide what the 100 tonners were. One of the 25 tonners of M.R.S. was taxed as a private motorcar because it was illogical to regard a petrol lorry as a locomotive. In the post-war years BLH 21 was taxed on its tractor weight of 11 tons 6 cwt at £145. Pickfords were taken to court but exonerated. For some reason KD 9168 was taxed on its total tractor plus trailer weight of 29 tons 15 cwt, the bill being £565.

The two 100 tonners carried a wide variety of loads in their lifetimes, for apart from traction engines, there were no other vehicles which could cope with even half their loads. The most common jobs were transporting locomotives from the makers such as Beyer Peacock of Manchester, Vulcan of Newton-le-Willows and Kitson of Leeds to Liverpool docks for export. One of the later tasks for BLH 21, in January 1951, was to take a diesel locomotive from Newton-le-Willows to London for the Festival of Britain. Other tasks included carrying transformers, presses for car manufacture, steel castings and, on one occasion, an 85 ton stranded whale.

The heaviest load was a 165 ton ingot mould carried by KD 9168 in December 1935 from the Brightside Foundry & Engineering Co of Sheffield to the Vickers Works of the English Steel Corporation, also in Sheffield. The journey was little over a mile, but icy conditions made the work difficult. Loading took three hours, during which time the lorry was blocking the Newhall Road tram lines; passengers alighted from a tram one side of the Scammell, walked around it and caught another on the other side. Average speed for the journey was 2 mph, and one occasion the driving wheels, struggling for grip, caused smoke to rise from the burning tarmac under them.

Both 100 tonners survive, KD 9168 in the British Commercial Vehicle Museum at Leyland, and BLH 21, still unrestored, at Rush Green Motors, Codicote, Hertfordshire.

Below: By January 1930 KD 9168 had received her number plate and was working for M.R.S. on one of their most regular jobs, carrying locomotives to Liverpool Docks. This one is for the North Western Railway of India. M.R.S. had a fleet of over 70 vehicles, many of them Scammells, capable of handling loads from 12 to 100 tons.

Above: A later photograph of KD 9168, showing changes in lettering of the headboard and dashboard. The man holding onto the nearside door may well have been the third member of the crew, often carried in addition to driver and steersman.

Below: Side, front and top elevation drawings of the 100 tonner tractor. In the top view, to the right of the steering wheel is a horizontal hand wheel used to actuate the brakes on the countershaft. There was also a transmission brake operated by pedal or small hand lever, the latter for re-starting on a hill. The front wheels were carried on conventional semi-elliptic springs, but at the rear springing was by vertical cylindrical rubber blocks. Behind them are coil rebound springs which acted as shock absorbers.

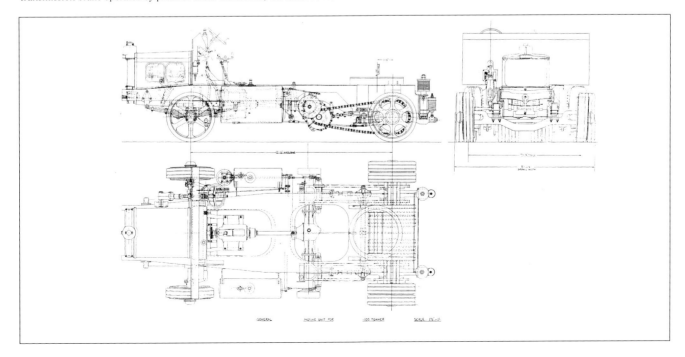

Left: In October 1931 M.R.S had the job of taking a 68 foot girder weighing 98 tons from Marylebone Goods Station to the site of the new Cumberland Hotel at Marble Arch. The vehicle consisted of a 100 ton tractor and trailer, to which was attached a sixteen wheel trailer, the whole outfit being 107 feet long. In order to choose the best route and ensure that all corners could be negotiated, a 1 inch to 1 foot scale Meccano model was made of the outfit, and tested on chalked plans of the roads, as shown here. Average speed for the journey was 1 mph, and at one point a traction engine was required to winch the trailer sideways.

Below: BLH 21 en route from Newton-le-Willows to the Festival of Britain site in London, with a diesel electric locomotive, in January 1951. It was operated by the Special Traffic (Pickfords) Division of British Road Services.

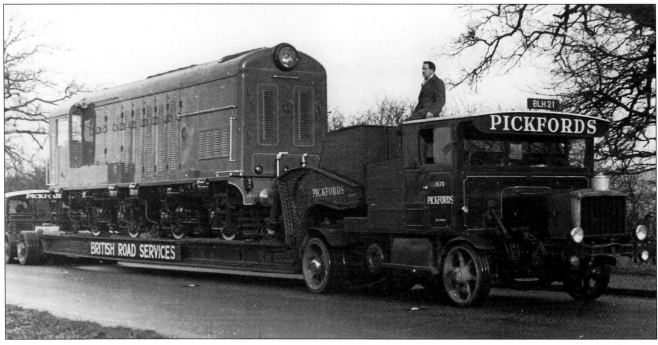

Below: Accommodation for the steersman varied greatly over the years. Here is KD 9168 at its first demonstration in November 1929. The steersman has a small seat, and can be seen talking into the Alfred Graham Admiralty type (sound powered, non-electric) telephone. Note the end of the quarter-elliptic spring projecting just below the trade plate. On a later version, *(below right)* the seat is facing forwards rather than sideways, and the steersman has some rudimentary weather protection.

Right: Record-breaking lorry and load - the lettering speaks for itself.

Below: This view of KD 9168 shows the heavy swan neck at the front of the carrier bed to which it was braced by a pair of hydraulic struts, one of which can be seen immediately in front of the boiler. These struts could raise or lower the bed by up to 15 inches, to clear road obstructions. The rubber suspension blocks, and below them the recoil springs, are visible behind the driving wheel. There was no other rear suspension on the tractor.

Bottom: By 1951 BLH 21 had a substantial cabin which could accommodate at least two men. If the load was too long, the cabin could be removed, and sometimes the telephone as well, in which case the steersman had to communicate by whistle. At least one photograph exists in which the platform has also been removed. As the outfits seldom travelled at more than walking speed this did not present problems for a short journey.

CHAPTER THREE

Rigids & Drawbar Tractors

Apart from the Pioneer 6x4 which was essentially designed for export and military markets (see Chapter 4), Scammell had built no rigid load carrying chassis until 1929. Announced as the 6 tonner, it was very similar to the articulated six wheelers, with wheelbase extended from 10ft to 14ft 3in or 17 feet. The same engine and gearbox featured, but chain drive gave way to an overhead worm rear axle with a final drive ratio of 7.75:1. This gave

Above and below: Although the 6- and 8-ton four-wheelers were announced with pneumatic tyres and overhead worm drive, a number were supplied with solids and chain drive, as here. The tipper is on the 14 ft 3 in wheelbase, while the wheelbase of the longer truck runs to 17 ft. Scammell would supply permutations on the four-wheeler theme, so there were also shaft-driven trucks on solids, and chain-drives with pneumatics.

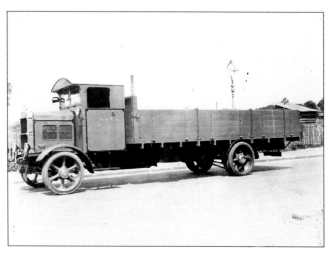

an overall top gear ratio of 13.5625:1, and a bottom gear ratio of 39.45:1. When it was announced in The Commercial Motor in October 1929, the 6 tonner was shown with shaft drive and pneumatic tyres, though some were made with chain drive and solids. Pneumatics were more popular, if only because of the advantage of a higher legal speed; 20 mph with pneumatics compared with 12 mph for solids.

For 1932 the 6 tonner was joined by an 8 tonner which used the same engine but had a deeper section frame and stronger springs. The standard tyres were 42x9 inch Goodyear pneumatics, though doubtless if a customer wanted solids he could have had them, for throughout its life the Scammell company would refuse no reasonable request for a special vehicle. Although chains were continued on some heavier tractors until shortly after World War 2, all newly-announced Scammell models used shaft drive after 1933. Front wheel brakes were a standard fitment, with the exception of the Mechanical Horse.

As on the tractors, a Gardner six-cylinder diesel engine was an alternative to the petrol, the diesels being easily recognised by their longer bonnets. A development of the four-wheelers, the 12-ton rigid six was a new model for 1933. This had a body space 21 feet long, normally used the Gardner 6LW engine and a six-speed gearbox, and initially had chain drive from a countershaft to the leading rear axle. This gave way to shaft drive on the 1934 models. The most interesting feature of the rigid 6-wheeler was the suspension of the rear axles. In place of steel springs, two parallel balance beams were pivoted at their centre to the ends of a cross member below the chassis frame, and at the rear end of the beams were two sets of rubber discs in compression which absorbed the road shocks. This suspension was also used on the trailer of the articulated eight wheeler, though with sets of rubber discs at both ends of the beams. A smooth ride was aided by large section single tyres all round. Other features of the specification included a constant-mesh six-speed gearbox and Dewandre compressed air braking system.

Although initially announced as a 12 tonner, the six-wheeler was capable of carrying at least 13 tons, and soon came to be known by this figure. With a chassis and body weight of 5 tons 18 cwt and a payload, with driver, passenger and fuel, of 13 tons 5 cwt, a diesel-engined six-wheeler averaged 10.5 mpg on a 157 mile run from London to Cardiff. Another oil-engined model, with 1007 cases of

baked beans weighing 12 tons 18 cwt, averaged 12 mpg on a 133 mile run from Bristol to Plymouth. So popular did the six-wheeler become for long-distance trunking work that the four wheeler was largely eclipsed from the mid-1930s onwards. Well-known companies who ran six-wheelers included Fisher Renwick, Pickfords, Whitbread and Wynns.

Short wheelbase four wheelers continued to be made for work as tractors with drawbar trailers, and two variants of this model were the timber tractor and Showtrac. The former was introduced in 1938, and used the 4-cylinder petrol engine and chain drive. A massive land anchor was mounted amidships under the chassis, and a crane with capacity of 2 tons was mounted at the rear.

The Showtrac was unusual in that it was the only internal combustion vehicle offered new to showmen for fairground work. Earlier, several traction engine makers had built showmen's locomotives, but otherwise showmen relied, as they still do, on ex-commercial and military vehicles. Scammell's links with the fairground began in 1933 when Jacob Studt asked the works to convert his chain-driven petrol-engined tractor to Gardner diesel power. Several other showmen followed his example; in 1938 J.W. Hoadley took delivery of a Gardner-powered chain-driven tractor with Mawdsley dynamo. It towed three trailers, and Mr. Hoadley reckoned that running costs were 50% less than those of a steamer. Road speed was higher, fuel cheaper and there were no delays for taking on coal and water. After the war the change from steam to diesel power accelerated. Demand exceeded supply, even

with the large numbers of ex-military vehicles which were coming onto the market, and anyway the American machines such as Federal, Mack, and Diamond T were petrol powered.

Scammell saw that there was a gap to be filled, and as early as 1945 they offered the Showtrac as a catalogued model. It was based on a standard LA-type 20-ton drawbar tractor powered by a 102 bhp Gardner 6LW engine. The last two Showtracs had Meadows 6 DC630 engines. While this was faster on the road than the Gardner, when it came to generating power on site the Gardner came into its own. Transmission was by a Scammell six-speed constant-mesh gearbox and shaft drive; an axle ratio of 11.28:1 gave a top speed of 28 mph. A 450 Amp dynamo by Mawdsley of Dursley was generally fitted though a few had Mather & Platt dynamos. The body was a specially-designed coachbuilt steel construction, built by Brown Bros of Tottenham, and returned to Scammell for painting and lettering. They had roller shutters on each side, and two rear doors.

One agent was appointed to supply Showtracs, Sidney Harrison Ltd of Bury St. Edmunds, Suffolk. Mr Harrison knew the fairground world well, for he had been a sales representative for Fowler when they were building showmen's engines. A total of eighteen Showtracs were supplied by Harrisons, the first in December 1945, the last in September 1948. These were the only genuine Showtracs, though a number of other tractors, including chain-driven models, were sold new by Scammell for fairground work.

Above: An 8-tonner on pneumatics with a drawbar trailer which raised the payload to 12 tons. The downside of this was a speed restriction of 12 mph, the same as if it had been a rigid truck on solids. The short bonnet indicates a petrol engine, which gave around 85 bhp at this date, so it would have been hard worked to cope with its 12 ton load. The cast steel wheels with ventilation holes for cooling the brake drums were standard on the new four wheelers, though not used on the solid tyred versions.

Above: An early example of a transit concrete mixer on a shaft-driven 6-ton chassis dating from 1931.

Right inset: chain-driven six wheeler tanker on the shorter wheelbase. Chain-drive models had the old four-speed gearbox, soon to give way to the constant mesh six speeder.

Below: An early six wheeler with chain drive to the leading rear axle. Originally known as the 12 tonner, they were soon rated at 13 tons capacity, and were known by this figure up to the end of production in 1939. In October 1933 it was reported that chain drive had given way to shaft, though doubtless some chain-driven models were still supplied to those who wanted them. The leaf springs at the rear gave way to Scammell's patent rubber suspension on the shaft driven six wheelers, but the tapered frame was retained.

Right: This Motor Transport advertisement of January 1934 referred to the 1933 Road Traffic Act which placed a heavy tax burden on vehicles with an unladen weight of more than four tons. With a platform body the Scammell six wheeler just scraped under the 4 ton limit, yet had a load capacity of 13 tons.

Below: The longer bonnet of this six wheeler indicates an 8.4-litre Gardner 6LW diesel engine. Available from 1932 the Gardner gave 102 bhp compared with the petrol unit's 85 bhp. Fuel consumption was 10.5 mpg over a varied 157 mile run from London to Cardiff.

Opposite right & above: Two petrol-engined shaft-drive six wheelers, a tipper for the London, Midland and Scottish Railway, and a van for the well-known carriers Fisher Renwick. Originally established as coastal ship operators under the name Manchester-London Steamers Ltd, they turned to road transport in the 1920s. They had a wharf on the Thames but their major base was at Muswell Hill, a depot which is still in existence. Their Manchester base was a very modern depot at Trafford Park, which was demolished some years ago. Note the individual name, "Sheldrake" on the Fisher Renwick van. The overall length of the six wheeler was 30 feet, and the body space from back of cab to end of frame, 22 feet 6 inches. Tyres were 13.5 x 16 inches all round.

Right: Several six-wheeled vans were supplied to the Stores Department of the General Post Office, and also at least one with open dropside bodywork. They were operated from Studd Street, London, and Birmingham. Note the oil side lamps for use when the van was stationary, a feature of other Post Office vehicles. The body had a roller blind door on the near side. The GPO had 13 big Scammells, rigid and articulated models, delivered between 1927 and 1940.

Left: An uncharacteristic and short-lived episode was Scammell's involvement in fire engines. The first to be delivered went to a local brigade, Watford, in early 1933. It had the familiar 85 bhp petrol engine, four-speed gearbox and worm drive rear axle. Equipment included a two-stage centrifugal pump made by J. Stone & Co of Deptford, London SE 14, and driven from an auxiliary gearbox mounted half way down the chassis. There was a Bayley's 55 foot telescopic ladder. With 130 feet of 2 inch hose and one jet from a 1 inch nozzle, a height of 139 feet was claimed. When the engine was being demonstrated at Uxbridge, the jet was 15 feet short of this figure. The sales manager instructed Frank Goodwin who worked on the engine side to put things right. After lunch the claimed figure was reached, and on the way home Frank was asked what he had done. "I'd lose my job if I told you," he said, but on being pressed admitted than he had taken a hacksaw and removed two blades of the fan. He kept his job, but Scammell sold no more fire engines of that design, despite submitting tenders to various brigades such as Finchley, Enfield, Ilford, Eastbourne, West Bromwich and other towns. The Watford engine remained in service until 1960.

Left: In May 1935 a second fire engine, named Silver Jubilee was supplied to Watford. Its engine was mounted further forward in the frame, there was now a six-speed constant-mesh gearbox and double reduction rear axle. In place of the earlier machine's straight frame, Silver Jubilee had a dropped centre section frame swept up over the rear axle; this gave a lower centre of gravity. Dewandre compressed air brakes were used, pressure being maintained by a Scammell-built two-cylinder compressor. Only one of this type was made, and was retained by Watford Fire Brigade until 1960.

Right: A typical drawbar tractor, an LA-type, delivered to London's Metropolitan Water Board in 1942. These were made for essential civilian purposes throughout the war, and were basically the same chassis as the motive units for semi-trailer work. In place of the turntable there was a robust ballast box of steel and timber construction. Later models had aluminium panelled sides or all-steel construction. Note the rear-mounted winch and spud. This illustration was used in the 1949 catalogue, described as the Medium Duty Tractor for loads of 100,000 pounds (44.6 tons).

Below: A 1946-registered tractor operated by John McCall of Kilmarnock, towing a 41ft 6in or 50ft Air Sea Rescue Launch made by British Power Boats or possibly Vospers. Note the auxiliary axle with larger tyres behind the three-axle trailer.

Right: Drawbar tractors could be supplied with either chain or shaft drive. The latter were more common from the mid 1930s onwards. This is a chain-drive model used for shunting railway wagons. It has a strange mixture of wheels, American-type bolt-on at the front, and cross-country track-grip rear tyres. The white painted extremities indicate wartime use.

Right and above: A Pickfords Highwayman tractor of 1958, with the wrap-around windscreen first seen that year, and cycle-type front wings which turned with the wheels. This was a characteristic of Pickfords' tractors, seen first on the 6x6 Constructor of 1952. The wing could be fitted much closer to the tyre, which was very useful in confined spaces, or where the vehicle had to negotiate uneven ground. The wings were smaller than the usual mudguards, so did not protrude on corners. The Highwayman tractor could be supplied as a dual-purpose machine, with a turntable for semi-trailer work, and ballast box with rear towing member, which could be mounted over the turntable. Pickfords tractors were often ballasted up for short-haul work. The tractors were rated as 20 or 25 tonners, but could pull loads up to 55 tons or more. The location of the 1960s view of a similar vehicle, XXW 906 with its Crane float trailer is the 'Sands' car park in Carlisle. An ERF of Reddish, Stockport-based Edward Beck & Sons Ltd., is parked alongside, its low loader carrying a new piece of Caterpillar plant.

Above: The drawbar tractors continued in production throughout the 1950s, being offered with Leyland 600 or 680 engines (125 or 150 bhp) or the Gardner 6LX 150. This Leyland 680-powered tractor, supplied to Pickfords in 1957, has the squared front wings introduced in the early 1950s. It is pulling part of a petrochemical processing plant. The dual language instructions on the front 'To be ventilated before entry - estar ventilado antes entrando' indicate a Spanish or Latin-American destination.

Left: A 20 ton drawbar tractor, on which has been mounted a wooden mock-up of the proposed generator to be used on the Showtrac. The actual generators were mounted on a specially sloped ballast block to allow for the propeller shaft drive from the p.t.o. Ahead of the generator is the 10-ton capacity winch fitted to Showtracs and to 20, 25 and latterly 30-ton capacity Highwayman tractors. Behind the winch is a form of spooling roller for the rope, which also passed through rollers incorporated in the rear-mounted drawbar cross member not yet fitted to this vehicle. The winch was part mounted under the mate's bench seat which was a boxed affair built into the rear of the cab, with a foam-filled seat for two persons.

Right: Showtrac number 6, delivered to Hibble & Mellors Ltd in June 1946. It replaced their Foster showman's engine, and was used mostly with Mellors' Super Dodgems, though sometimes with an Orton-Spooner-built Waltzer. Like a number of Showtracs it was supplied with easy-fit tracks for coping with slippery ground. It was sold to E.L. Morley in 1964 and retired in 1973.

Above: The third Showtrac made, delivered new to Arnold Brothers in May 1946, and sold to Thomas Benson & Son in 1960, in whose service it is seen here at Hampstead Heath in April 1965. Bensons were still using it in the late 1970s. Several well known showmen used to pay for their Showtracs in pound notes, with as many as 3,000 or more, spread out on the desk. The driver collecting the Showtrac received a bonus of £1, later raised to £5.

Right: Scammell Showtrac DDT 181 'West Riding' first registered in June 1946. Chassis 6173, it was fitted with a Mather & Platt dynamo. It is pictured here in 1969 after being bought from original purchaser Frank Harniess and receiving full restoration by its new owner Harry Wigfield. This vehicle passed into the hands of Scammell enthusiast Roger Austin in 1990.

CHAPTER FOUR

Cross Country, Military and Export, The Pioneer and its Descendants

In June 1927 Scammell literally entered new territory when they built the prototype of a rigid six wheeler intended as a cross-country vehicle. Not much attention had been given by British truck makers to cross-country performance, because there was little need for it at home, and the industry was not geared up to building special vehicles for export. However Scammell had their eyes on these markets, and also military needs, and it was with this in mind that they built a prototype of their rigid six wheeler, later named the Pioneer.

In appearance it differed from other Scammells then being made in having a radiator set back further in the frame, and later it was to become even more distinctive with its 'coffee pot' header tank above the radiator. The engine was the standard 7-litre four-cylinder unit, quoted in 1927 as giving 65 bhp. The gearbox was the standard four-speed unit, but it was in the drive to the rear wheels that real ingenuity was shown. It was the work of Oliver Danson North (1887-1968), who was the inspiration behind so much of Scammell's thinking between 1923, when he joined the firm, and his retirement in 1948. He avoided the

complexities of twin differentials and driving axles by using a single Kirkstall overhead worm axle and two conventional halfshafts. At the end of each were spur pinions which meshed with idler wheels in front and behind it, these in turn meshing with spur wheels on two short shafts which carried the driving wheels.

Each of the cases carrying the train of gears was free to rock on the axle, allowing one wheel to rise as much as two feet above its fellow wheel on the same side, with both wheels still being driven. Suspension was by long semi-elliptic springs on each side, while front suspension was by a transverse semi-elliptic spring pivoted at the centre. The tyres were much larger than any which had been seen on Scammells before, 44x10 inch straight-sided Goodyear pneumatics. They were rated to carry 2 tons each, or a total of 12 tons. The chassis weighed 5 tons, allowing for a body plus load weight of 7 tons; the Pioneer was described as a 5 to 7 tonner.

On test the Pioneer proved capable of feats never seen before. It climbed out of a pit with sides 3ft 6in high with all six wheels remaining in contact with the ground, and

Left: The second prototype rigid six wheeler (not yet named Pioneer) fitted with tracks on the driving wheels. It was intended for oilfield work in Venezuela, carrying long pipes and steel derrick members up to 35 feet, hence the narrow cab allowing pipes to be carried on either side of it.

Right: An early Pioneer with a simple test body, possibly a demonstration model for the Army. Although the articulated tank transporter was not built until 1932, the Army did look at some rigid chassis as early as 1929, and in the Second World War they bought more tractors than tank transporters.

driven at speed against a 2ft bank it reared up with front wheels about 4ft in the air, yet the rear wheels climbed the bank. A later 6x6 version climbed the vertical wall of the factory, the rear bogie supplying forward pressure while the front wheels climbed to over 7 feet. The rear articulation was such that even with the front wheels at this height, the rear four were all on the ground.

Interesting, in view of the fact that Scammell never built passenger vehicles, was a design for a low-loading 6x4 bus chassis using O.D. North's patent bogie drive. Announced at the same time as the truck, it had a bevel drive rear axle with a ground clearance of only seven inches, and a two foot floor height.

The first two rigid six wheelers (the name Pioneer did not come into use until later) were supplied for oilfield work in Venezuela. Customers did not come swarming to Watford, and it was not until 1932 that a sizable order was received. By this time the familiar 'coffee pot' above a staggered row of wire-wound tubes had been adopted; this ensured that at whatever angle the truck leaned, the ends of the water tubes would always remain covered. The order came from the Iraq Petroleum Company who were

developing the Mosul oilfield. From Kirkuk to the coastal outlets at Haifa and Tripoli the pipes ran for 1500 miles, and it was to transport these 40 to 50 foot long pipes that the company turned to Scammell. Most previous Pioneers had been load-carrying chassis, but for oilfield work they were used as tractive units with a central box section girder semi-trailer. The two axles at the rear of the trailer were carried on a separate girder, which could be slid along the central member to vary the trailer length. Iraq Petroleum ordered 21 of these Pioneers, starting a long tradition of Scammells in Middle Eastern oilfield work.

Pioneers were also used as tankers by the Anglo-Persian Oil Company and by Shell in Australia where a rigid six pulled a four wheeled drawbar trailer, and as general load carriers by South African Roadways of Durban. By 1931 there was an Argentine branch, Camiones Scammell. In 1934 a 6x6 Pioneer was sold to Siemens of Berlin for work in undeveloped countries. This had a five-speed gearbox; this and the six-speeder were available on Pioneers during the 1930s. At least one Pioneer was supplied for oilfield work in Rumania, in 1938. Relatively few were sold on the home market, though the Newcastle-on-Tyne Electric

Right: The British Army's first Pioneer tank transporter supplied to the RAOC in 1932. It is carrying a Vickers Medium Mark 2 tank which weighed 13 tons, less than a quarter of the Challenger's weight, carried by Scammell Commanders in the 1980s. Note that it carries a civilian registration, MV 5364.

Left: One of the first 6x6 Pioneers, an artillery tractor for the Indian Army, c.1929. It is equipped with a 6-ton horizontal drum winch.

Supply Co Ltd had two and Edinburgh Corporation Electricity Department at least one.

The other obvious use for the Pioneer was a military one, but the early 1930s were a lean period for this market. Very little money was spent on equipping the armed forces, and although the Army was always ready to test prototype vehicles, no large orders resulted. The first Scammell supplied against a military order was a second-hand motive unit (ex-E.W. Rudd) in 1926, and the first new vehicle was a Pioneer chassis with dropped frame at the front and lowered radiator supplied in May 1928, to be fitted with an armoured car body.

From the first appearance of tanks in 1915, the accepted operation was for them to be taken by rail as near to the battle front as possible, and then travel under their own power. However the railways were vulnerable to damage and all too often went nowhere near where the tanks were needed. These were slow travelling under their own power,

Below: A demonstration of the flexibility of the Pioneer's rear bogies.

and frequently broke down before they reached the battle zone. The French Army had used Knox tractors with semi-trailers for tank transport in the last years of the war, but apart from an AEC with Bauly trailer which carried Holt caterpillar tractors, the British Army had nothing until 1932 when Scammell supplied a Pioneer with low-loading semi-trailer to the Royal Army Ordnance Corps. The two-axle bogie was detachable, with knock-out axles, but instead of having separate side jacks as on the civilian models, the bogie incorporated its own screw jacks which were wound up and down manually. Only four of this design were built, later ones having the more sensible arrangement of a ramp up which the tanks could be driven under their own power to a carrying platform above the bogie.

The self-loading design appeared in 1939, just in time for the Second World War, and went into immediate production. 548 Pioneers were made for tank transport, and proved invaluable, both in the sand of the Western Desert and the mud of Northern Europe. There were few tight spots which a Pioneer could not get itself and other vehicles out of. Its chief drawback was very heavy steering, not helped by muddy conditions, and it often required two men to pull the wheel round. When the electric starter failed, it was the job of three men to get the engine going, one on the handle and two pulling a rope looped over it.

Early military Pioneers had Scammell 4-cylinder engines, but all wartime ones were Gardner-powered, and used the six-speed constant mesh gearbox. The 20 ton trailers were made by Scammell, but later 30 tonners were made by Shelvoke & Drewry as well as Scammell. The S & D design was originally for use with the Diamond T 980 tractor, and incorporated counterbalanced loading ramps designed by James Drewry, that could be operated by one man. Pioneers were also used as heavy recovery tractors and artillery tractors. The former had a Herbert Morris sliding jib 2-ton crane. They could be fitted with tracks over the rear wheels.

Pioneer production came to an end in 1945, but the design was adapted to civilian use in Scammell's 80-ton tractor. These had wider cabs with ample crew accommodation, and were made only as ballast-box tractors for the heaviest loads. They shared the really heavy haulage work for firms such as Pickfords, E.W. Rudd and Red House Motor Services with the ex-army Diamond Ts and the old Scammell 100 tonners which were used up to 1953. Ex-military Pioneers were also used in large numbers for heavy hauling all over the world, and remained popular with showmen well into the 1970s. One was still in use as a yard tractor in Antwerp, pulling 60 ton loads, in 1990. It has now been bought for preservation. Some of the heavy recovery and showmen's Pioneers had rebuilt or new bodies which made them virtually unrecognisable.

The Pioneer's replacement was the Explorer, developed from a 6x6 version of the Pioneer. Six wheel drive was needed because of the Army's demand for even greater cross-country ability, and because most other Army vehicles used petrol fuel, the Explorer had a 10.35-litre Meadows unit which gave 200 bhp, a great improvement over the 102 bhp Gardner 6LW. The 6 DC650 engine left the Meadows factory as a diesel, as used in Scammell's rigid-eight wheeler, and was modified for petrol fuel by Scammell, with new cylinder heads and pistons. Mick Green remembers the engines being tested, running at full revs for hours on end. Watford's small engine test house had only two beds, and testing of Scammell's other 'home produced engine', that of the Mechanical Horse, suffered as a consequence. In this form the Meadows was known as the 6 PC650 (650 cubic inches). The fuel consumption of 2 to 3 mpg did not worry the military particularly, and the Explorers did not see the regular daily use of civilian tractors. The few that passed

into civilian hands were usually converted to diesel power, with an improvement to about 12 mpg.

The Pioneer had introduced Scammell to the oil industry, and in the post-war years they supplied a considerable number of specialised vehicles. Introduced in 1949, the Mountaineer was a 4x4 with the transverse leaf front suspension of the Pioneer, powered by the same 10.35 litre Meadows engine as the Explorer. It was made as a short-wheelbase dump truck, (see Chapter Seven), a long-wheelbase load carrier and as a tractor trailer unit. Later in the 1950s, the Mountaineer could be had with Leyland, Gardner or Rolls-Royce engines. Not all Mountaineers were for oilfield work; the dump trucks were used for road construction and other civil engineering undertakings in Britain, while drawbar tractors were used by Pickfords and Wynns for smaller loads than those requiring the 80-tonner or Constructor tractors.

Above and right: These front views of the Pioneer give a good idea of the remarkable flexibility of the suspension. The single transverse spring at the front was continued on the Mountaineer and Constructor. Note also the wirewound vertical tubes of the Still radiator and the 'coffee pot' tank which prevented the tops of the tubes from becoming uncovered, whatever extraordinary angle the Pioneer might adopt.

Left: Even in the early days, not all oilfield Scammells were Pioneers. This is a narrow-cab four wheeler of 1928, for use in the Maracaibo region of Columbia, South America. It had a winch mounted behind the cab and the Still radiator like that of the Pioneer, though without the 'coffee pot'.

Below left: In 1929 The Commercial Motor observed that 'the rigid six wheeler is not seen on British roads in large numbers,' but one customer was Edinburgh Corporation Electricity Department. Other domestic users of the six wheeler included the Newcastle-on-Tyne Electrical Supply Co, who used theirs, as no doubt did Edinburgh, for taking electric motors to outlying rural districts with no metalled roads.

Below: In 1935 Scammell supplied two special Pioneer tractors with 4250 gallon Thompson frameless tanker trailers to the Anglo-Iranian Oil Company. They were intended for distribution of petrol from the refinery at Kermanshah to depots all over Iran, reaching altitudes of 10,000 feet. While off-road work was not generally envisaged, they had to be ready to leave metalled roads at times. Neither the 85 bhp Scammell petrol engine or the 102 bhp Gardner diesel gave enough power, so Scammell chose a petrol-fuelled straight-8 Parsons marine engine which gave 168 bhp from nearly 14 litres. It was modified for road work, with Scammell-designed cylinder heads. The extra length of this engine accounted for the tractor's distinctive appearance, though most other components were shared with the Pioneer. However, instead of the transverse leaf front suspension, Gruss air springs mounted on a cross-bar shackled to conventional longitudinal semi-elliptics were used. It even had a primitive form of sleeper cab, for 'provision is made for a man to sleep, lying fore and aft, on the floor of the cab at the near side.'

Above: The Recovery Tractor version of the Pioneer was officially the SV2S (the Heavy Artillery Tractor was the R100 and the tank transporter the TRMU/30 or TRCU/30). It had a Herbert Morris crane with sliding jib.

Below: Two Pioneer R100s coupled to a three-axle trailer carrying a 14¼-ton Cruiser A13 Mark III tank. The R100, which was mainly used as an artillery tractor, had accommodation for a crew of nine.

Left: Another demonstration of the remarkable front axle articulation of the Pioneer. Headlights on these military Pioneers were mounted lower than on the civilian models. This artillery tractor chassis is being tested with chains on the rear wheels.

Below: The Pioneer was second to none in coping with really difficult conditions, but this one seems to be receiving assistance itself, judging from the towing cable at the front. The vehicle is coupled to a 30-ton tank transporter trailer carrying a Matilda tank.

Above: Most ex-military Pioneers were used either as recovery vehicles by garage proprietors and transport companies, as heavy haulage tractors or with showmen, but this is a rare example of a tipper with Edbro equipment by Edwards Brothers Ltd of Bolton, Lancs.

Above and below: This Pioneer found its way to New Zealand where it was engaged in hauling a double-ended canoe-style MFV (Motor Fishing Vessel). It required the assistance of a 4x4 tractor-shovel, probably a Caterpillar, on Saddle Hill.

Above: Pioneers were popular with showmen in the post-war years, many surviving in the fairgrounds for more than 20 years after being demobbed. This one, operated by Edwards of Swindon and named Queen Elizabeth II, was photographed in the Cotswold village of Broad Campden in 1967.

Left: This ex-W.D. Pioneer saw civilian service with Hobbs Quarries of Bristol. Photographed in 1967, it was rebuilt in the company's own workshops and fitted out with heavy lifting and towing equipment, jacks and cutting gear. It was based at their Nailsea depot and used by their repair section for all recovery work.

Above and below: After the war Scammell continued to make tractors of Pioneer type, differing from the Army version mainly in having wider cabs. As built by Scammell, they had only two doors, though at least one four-door cab, built on an ex-military Pioneer, was operated by Pickfords. Scammell called their new model the Heavy Duty Tractor, 'a 190,000 pound tractor for hauling abnormal loads on drawbar trailers over soft or bad ground'. The capacity is equivalent to 84.82 tons, and they were commonly known as 80 tonners, though some hauled gross combination weights near to 150 tons. As well as the Wimpey operated tractor shown here, they were used by Pickfords, Edward Box and Red House Motor Services. The second view shows the tractor undergoing maintenance in the Wimpey workshops alongside one of the company's 'box' tractors.

Opposite page: Two examples of Pickford's fleet of 80 ton Scammell Pioneers are pictured here on the North Circular Road, Finchley in the early 1950s pulling and pushing a large refinery vessel, on solid tyred bogies built by Crane but designed by Dyson, to the Mobilgas Vacuum Oils Coryton refinery, Essex. These dependable but slow ballast tractors were the mainstay of the company's heavy haulage operations in the post-war period. They were eventually to give way to the Constructor range of models, the first of many examples joining the company's fleet in February 1955. The lower picture depicts chassis no. 6449, prior to entering service in June 1948, the vehicle's pleasing lines being enhanced by Pickford's livery and lining.

Above: Production of the genuine Pioneer ended in 1945, but work soon started on its replacement. Army needs dictated a six-wheel-drive vehicle, which was not new to Scammell, who had made their first 6x6 Pioneer in 1929. A wartime Pioneer with a driven front axle was extensively tested, and became, in effect the prototype of the Explorer. Production Explorers shared the Pioneer's suspension, front and rear, and the six-speed constant mesh gearbox. They were supplied mainly for military use (this is a batch of twenty three for the British Army in 1950), and some export models had engine variations. Those for the Egyptian Army had Rolls-Royce C6NFL diesels, and those for New Zealand were also diesel powered, with Meadows 6 DC630s.

Right: One of two Explorer recovery tractors of the RAF's 51 MT Squadron in Egypt in 1955.

Above: A British Army Explorer demonstrates its recovery ability as it suspends tows this Bedford QLT 3-ton 4x4 troop carrier. Although its lift capacity was a modest 3-tons, the 6x6 tractor had immense off-road capabilities and was well suited for the task of recovering soft-skin and wheeled armoured vehicles. Unlike its predecessor, however, there was not such a ready market for the Explorer by the time the first examples were being discharged into civilian life in the late 1960s. This was now the age of the motorway and the 13-ton petrol driven tractor with outdated equipment was not an attractive proposition, furthermore many examples of the ex-WD Pioneer still remained operational – these vehicles after all, were built to last.

Above left: A Royal Engineer attached Explorer. Of interest are the huge ground anchors in the raised position at the rear of the vehicle. In this instance they cannot be used whilst the vehicle sits astride the railway track so the crew have resorted to Heath Robinson principles and wedged a plank between the rear wheels to stop it sliding back during winching operations.

Left: Four diesel-engined Explorers were supplied to the New Zealand Army in 1959. They had the later type front bumper and wings, and could be fitted with tracks on the rear bogie to improve traction on difficult ground.

Right and below: Scammell's first post-war export vehicles were a series of 4x2s for oilfield work, introduced in 1946. Made in three wheelbase lengths, a 10 ft tractor and trucks of 16 and 18 feet, they used the same Meadows petrol engines as the Explorer, detuned to 190 bhp, and had characteristic low bonnets and exhaust pipes angled to discharge horizontally over the cab roof. The Pioneer-type 'coffee pot' radiators were used, and other features included a power take off from the transmission, double reduction rear axle and compressed air braking. Most went to South America (this 4x2 tipper was for exploration by Shell in the Maracaibo region of Columbia) though some were sold to the Middle East.

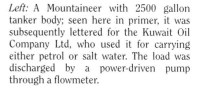

Above: A long-wheelbase (19ft) Mountaineer, one of several built in 1952 for carrying locust bait in Saudi Arabia. The sites of swarms were spotted from aeroplanes, and the bait was taken by truck and laid at night. The Mountaineers could be used solo, or with a 10-ton trailer.

Left: A Mountaineer with 2500 gallon tanker body; seen here in primer, it was subsequently lettered for the Kuwait Oil Company Ltd, who used it for carrying either petrol or salt water. The load was discharged by a power-driven pump through a flowmeter.

Left: A later Mountaineer, from the mid 1950s, with the front wings fixed to the frame, instead of swinging with the wheels.

Above: This Mountaineer began life as an articulated tractor for the Royal Air Force, but on 'demob' it was acquired by Hills of Botley, Hants. It is seen here in 1966 at Boldre Wood in the New Forest, being loaded with timber destined to become radar masts. These are carried on two separate bogies. The crane is mounted on an ex-military AEC chassis.

Left: An articulated timber transporter with a 14ft wheelbase Mountaineer tractor and 25 ton extensible pole trailer. It was built for Steel Brothers of Tanganyka in 1951.

Below: Among the largest passenger vehicles ever made these are 126-seater Sparshatt/ Rollalong bodies with Mountaineer motive units, built for the Middle East in 1962.

CHAPTER FIVE

The Lighter Side: Autovan and Mechanical Horse

Up to 1927 Scammell had concentrated on the heavier end of the truck world, but they then decided to explore the large market for short-haul delivery vans. This had been largely cornered by American makes such as Chevrolet and Ford (the latter assembled in Manchester), though 1924 saw a strong domestic challenger in the 1-ton Morris Commercial. All these designs were conventional, but the machine that O.D. North and Percy Hugh came up with was far from it. North had always been fascinated by the radial engine, which had been a feature of the 5-cylinder North-Lucas car which he had designed in 1922. In the Scammell Autovan the engine was a 3-cylinder unit, air-cooled and mounted under the driver's seat. This was directly over the front axle, which was driven via a vertical shaft to the 3-speed gearbox and thence to a worm gear and two double universally jointed shafts to the stub axles of the front wheels.

The forward-control Autovan bore some resemblance to the Shelvoke & Drewry Freighter which had been in production since 1922, but that had a transverse water cooled engine. A nearside-mounted radiator gave adequate cooling, but this was the downfall of the Autovan, which overheated badly, especially when stationary in traffic, which it was likely to be by the nature of its work. Only four Autovans were made, and it never went on sale.

Oliver North was not quite through with radial engines, for in 1929 he designed an armoured car using the Pioneer's rear suspension and a rear-mounted radial engine. It never got beyond the model stage, unlike his next unconventional design, which was one of the most successful solutions to the problems of moving goods in confined spaces. This came about through an initiative from the railway companies. Traditionally the enemies of road transport, the four railway companies nevertheless operated a large number of light vehicles carrying parcels, food, beer and other goods from about 2000 depots to retail outlets. In 1930 much of this work was still undertaken by horse and cart. These had the advantage of manoeuvrability in narrow streets and yards, and ability to change easily from one cart to another, but they were slow, and the number of men familiar with horses was shrinking. The L.M.S. (London, Midland and Scottish) Railway cooperated with Karrier in the design of a light three-wheeled tractor powered by a Jowett flat-twin engine, and the L.N.E.R. (London and North Eastern Railway) planned a similar machine, though with a four-cylinder engine, with Napier.

The old-established Napier company was at a cross roads in 1931. Their managing director Montague Napier died suddenly, and a caretaker management decided to re-enter the road vehicle field, which they had abandoned for aero engines seven years earlier. Two projects were undertaken, a luxury car for which they hoped to secure the service of W.O. Bentley as designer, and the Mechanical Horse. A prototype was built, with a 2-litre engine designed in house, and an automatic coupling system for the semi-trailer. It worked well during its first trials, but it seems

Left: Front end of the Autovan, showing the starting handle for the air-cooled radial engine, inboard brakes and solid tyres. The rear wheels, also with solid tyres, were considerably smaller. Front suspension was independent by two transverse leaf springs.

Above: The prototype Mechanical Horse, which started life as a Napier, and became a Scammell during 1932. Though the bonnet is of the Napier type, it was shown in this form on the Scammell stand at the Scottish Motor Show in November 1932. The single headlamp on the offside was repeated on the first Scammells, though it was soon moved to the nearside. Note the Klaxon horn which was not generally continued by Scammell, though some operated by the railways did have them. Nor were the trailer's externally-mounted jockey wheels; these were located inboard of the tractor's wheels, between the chassis members, when O.D. North took over the design. However, some L.M.S. Scammell tractors did use the external wheels, known as the Wolverton system after the L.M.S. railway works where it was developed.

that neither management nor the engineering department were fond of the Mechanical Horse. P.J. Wallace, one of the latter, said most of the people engaged on the Mechanical Horse would have much preferred to be working on the luxury car. "Except for the man designing the engine, few hearts were in the job; as designers of aero engines we resented the indignity of 'slumming' among lorries. Among ourselves, we did not speak of the Mechanical Horse, but of the Mountain Goat, such was the measure of our contempt!"

After two or three prototypes had been made, Napier sold the whole Mechanical Horse project to Scammell for a few thousand pounds. Oliver North immediately got to work redesigning some aspects of it, though the basic Napier layout was retained. In addition to the 40 bhp 2-litre engine for a 5 tonner, North designed a smaller unit of 1125 cc and 29 bhp for 3 ton loads. Both were monobloc side valve units with gravity feed from a 6-gallon fuel tank, and were offset to the near side, together with the four-speed gearbox and final drive. The Scammell Mechanical Horse was announced in the press in November 1932, using a photograph of the Napier-built prototype, though there was no mention whatever of Napier's involvement. It seems that this prototype was displayed on the Scammell stand at the Glasgow Show in November 1932, for The Commercial Motor was at pains to point out that the outfit seen at the show was an experimental model, and production versions would have different specifications.

When it went into production in the Spring of 1933, the Mechanical Horse had a new cab with shorter, snub-nose bonnet which was little changed until the arrival of the Scarab in 1948. It was offered in three sizes, the 3- and 5-tonner sharing the smaller engine but having different rear axle ratios, and the 6 tonner with the 2-litre engine. The 5 tonner did not last long, but the others remained in production for fifteen years, and were known as the MH3 and MH6. A new, separate sales department was set up (MH), distinct from the heavy vehicles (HV). Each was a separate unit with its own sales managers reporting to the Managing Director. MH dealt through a distributor network for home and overseas orders, while HV sold direct to customers worldwide. The first large contract came from the L.N.E.R. who placed an order for 80 tractors and 113 trailers in April 1933.

Within a few years the Mechanical Horse was replacing the equine variety all over the country. Typical was the biscuit manufacturer, Peak Frean, whose last 12 horses were retired in May 1934, being replaced by five

Above: Although the L.N.E.R. was the inspiration behind the Napier design, this photo shows that at least one prototype was built for the L.M.S.

Above right: An early Scammell-built prototype, with the new snub-nosed bonnet designed by North. The doorless cab was inherited from Napier; production mechanical horses all had doors. This prototype, which bears the words 'Patent Applied For' on the chassis frame, is very close to the production models, with such features as the rounded front bumper and offset starting handle. The first production examples appeared in the Spring of 1933, quickly making inroads to the world of its equine counterpart.

Scammells. In the words of the company's forwarding manager, "They are going because we cannot afford slow motion in these days of rapid movement and prompt delivery of goods." Although the railways were the largest users of the Mechanical Horse, many other concerns bought them, brewers, paper makers, timber merchants, haulage contractors such as Thomas Allen and Hay's Wharf Cartage Co, and the Metropolitan Police who used a low-loading trailer to take away abandoned cars. The Mechanical Horse found many applications in municipal service, from refuse collectors to street washers, sweepers and gulley emptiers. Alternative motive powers appeared before long; a 2.75-litre Perkins Wolf diesel was available for 1938, as was an electric version with 9.5 hp motor and four-speed controller. The diesel could be operated with a single axle semi-trailer for loads up to 10 tons, or with two axles, 15 tons. The Great Western Railway were among customers. The electric versions were made in conjunction with Electricars of Birmingham, and Partridge, Wilson of Leicester and were employed almost exclusively on municipal work.

The Mechanical Horse was exported to many countries for a variety of work; examples were milk collection and refuse work in Malta, collecting sugar cane in Jamaica, and delivering meat for the Rangoon Meat Marketing Board. They were sold in France by Chenard-Walcker, and from 1937 were made there, being known as F.A.R.s. Originally very similar in appearance to the Scammells, they acquired more distinctive cabs after the war, and were made in various forms up to 1970. Some of the post-war F.A.R.s had Dyna-Panhard flat twin engines, recalling the 832 cc V-twin Scammell Mechanical Horse for two ton loads which the L.N.E.R. experimented with in 1938.

The Mechanical Horse was made until 1948, when it was replaced by the Scarab. This had a very different appearance, with a rounded front designed by Scammell and built for them by the Willenhall Radiator Company, using various pressings from the Bedford O Series lorry. Under the skin the Scarab was also greatly changed, as the engine was moved from its frontal position to the rear of the cab, where it was in unit with the

Left: An early production MH3 operated by Scammell's Manchester Service Depot. Registered towards the end of 1933, it has the mesh grille which soon gave way to the familiar slats.

Above: This view of the Mechanical Horse chassis shows the offset engine and transmission. Though necessary for space reasons, it made the vehicle somewhat unstable, and liable to tip over if cornered too enthusiastically to the right. A central engine position (behind the cab) was the single greatest improvement incorporated in the Scarab design. Note the 6 gallon fuel tank ahead of the steering wheel, and the ramps at the rear of the chassis for automatic coupling of the trailer.

Above: The motive unit with carrier coupled up, showing the jockey wheels in retracted position. When a hook was released and the motive unit driven away, the jockey wheels dropped into position by gravity. This was much neater than the Wolverton system of fixed jockey wheels, but sometimes the leg pivot did not work freely enough, and the jockey wheels failed to drop completely to support the carrier.

gearbox and rear axle. This had the effect of lowering the centre of gravity and increasing the weight on the rear axle for better traction. The engine was a new 2054 cc Scammell-built unit giving 25 bhp in the 3-ton model and 45 bhp in the 6 tonner. This was used in most of the 13,000 Scarabs built, though Perkins diesels became available in the mid 1950s. Like its predecessor, the Scarab was widely exported, forming the mainstay of municipal fleets of African cities such as Nairobi, Mombasa and Lagos.

In the 1960s Scarab sales began to drop, largely because British Railways were closing many of the depots and relying on larger vehicles making full-day journeys. Also the Scarab's top speed of below 30 mph was becoming inconvenient with higher traffic speeds generally. An updated three-wheeler called the Townsman took over in 1964. This replaced the 3-ton Scarab, though the 6-tonner was continued until 1967. The Townsman had a freshly-designed cab, now made of grp and built by Thornycroft, which was now, like Scammell, part of the Leyland group. The engine was a 2.6-litre Standard/Leyland OE 160, and hydraulic brakes were fitted, though only on the rear wheels. This brought about the eventual end of the mechanical horse, as Construction & Use Regulations of 1968 made braking on all wheels mandatory. They also insisted on dual-line air brakes on the semi-trailers, which required manual coupling and uncoupling. The Townsman would probably have had a relatively short life anyway, as the reasons for the decline in Scarab sales became more powerful in the late 1960s.

The final development of the mechanical horse theme was the Scarab Four, a four-wheeled tractor which used the cab of the Standard Atlas van combined with a modified Scarab engine/transmission/rear axle unit. It was more stable than the three-wheeler and had a more spacious cab, but did not sell well as it had none of the manoeuvrability

of the three wheelers. It was launched at the 1962 Commercial Motor Show but production did not get under way until 1964, and ended that year. Only 120 were made, though the design had a further short lease of life under the name Leyland 20.

Below: This 1934 advertisement from Motor Transport stresses the advantages of the Mechanical Horse over both the horse and the conventional lorry. The picture shows the mechanical horse on full lock; its turning circle was a remarkable 15 feet, 10 ft less than that of a London cab.

Left and below: These photos show variations in lighting equipment which make generalisations dangerous. Both are MH3s, the flatbed trailer for removal work dating from 1937, and the refuse collector from 1946. The latter has an offside headlamp and small side lamps, while the earlier example has the headlamp on the nearside, which was its more usual position, and no side lamps. Although only rated for 3 tons, the removal trailer has twin rear wheels.

This page: Scammell made much of their 'Four in Hand' system for municipal work, where one mechanical horse could operate with four different trailers, and still pay only one tax. The trailers were a bin carrier, moving floor refuse collector, gulley emptier and street washer. The bin carrier was a Scammell patented design, and employed six 1 cubic yard or three 2 cubic yard bins, each fitted with rubber tyred wheels so that they could be easily (and quietly) pushed around. A tipping angle of 55° ensured rapid emptying of the load. The moving floor refuse collector could be fitted with shafts if the operators wanted to use horses for door-to-door collection. The gulley emptier for Bognor Regis has a street sprinkler as well. The box over the rear axle contained a separate petrol engine and rotary pump for creating a vacuum in the sludge tank.

Left: The City of Westminster Cleansing Department operated 26 of these Scammell-Electricars, with wide three-seater cabs, with a variety of trailers for refuse collecting, gulley-emptying and street sprinkling. Introduced in 1937, they remained in operation until 1962, when they gave way to Dennis tractors, also battery powered. This gulley-emptier trailer is by Eagle of Warwick.

Left: Partridge, Wilson & Co of Leicester also made an electric version of the Mechanical Horse, seen here in chassis form. Lighter than the Electricars, it is still carrying a formidable complement of batteries.

Below: A Mechanical Horse with a drawbar trailer seems a contradiction, but some were made, including this ballast-box tractor with mobile library trailer, operated by the Borough of Acton in the 1950s. Before the war some Mechanical Horses had been used with four-wheeled trailers originally made for horse traction.

Above: This drawbar tractor was a 1934 MH3 geared down to pull six ton loads. It was never registered for the road (the number plate MH 6 is not a genuine registration) and never even had a chassis number. It worked well at speeds up to 15 mph, but was often driven at 25 mph or more, which led to overheating. Used around the Tolpits Lane factory until closure in 1988, it is now in the Commercial Vehicle Museum at Leyland.

Above: With the approach of the Second World War, Scammell produced a number of trailers for combating the effects of air raids. These included this poison gas decontamination vehicle, which could carry a squad of twelve men and their equipment, including stores of sand and lime, 100 gallons of water, bleach spreader, brooms, buckets, first aid outfit and stretcher. The canvas roof could be easily removed and spotlights raised to illuminate the scene. While the crew were dealing with the emergency, the tractor could return to base to collect a street-washing trailer.

Below: Another contribution to the war effort by Scammell was the manufacture of large numbers of fire pumps for A.R.P. (air raid precaution) work. Some were light enough to be carried by two men, or on a wheelbarrow type frame, others were 475 gallon per minute two wheeled trailer pumps, such as these being delivered to the Auxiliary Fire Service on a low-loading trailer.

Left: A Scammell trailer pump pulled by a Mechanical Horse fire engine. This carried its own water supply, a 300 gallon tank, a rotary pump driven from the engine, as well as a detachable two-man portable pump, and a 30 foot ladder. It could carry a crew of five, including the driver. Several were supplied for works use, including Scammell themselves and the Stewart & Lloyds steelworks. The 2-litre engine was used in the Trailer Fire Pump, for which a section was formed in 1939. Alan Baker remembers working there as a graduate trainee, and encountering problems in obtaining enough power to prime a 24ft suction lift in the required time, something like 20 seconds, using an exhaust-operated venturi-type ejector. Also working on the project under Chief Engineer P.C. Hugh was Harry Weslake, later famous for his work on the Jaguar XK120 engine and later still with Dan Gurney and his Weslake-powered Eagles in his All-American Racers Formula One team in the mid to late 1960s. A disagreement on cylinder head design between Hugh and Weslake led to a stand-up row ("Only just without fisticuffs" Baker recalls). In the end it was Hugh who backed off, wisely in view of Westlake's pre-eminence as a cyclinder head engineer.

Left and below: A lesser-known variant of the Mechanical Horse was the Trivan, a load-carrying three-wheeler with varying wheelbases. Load capacities and engines were as with the Mechanical Horse, 1125cc for 3 ton loads and 2043cc for the 6 tonner. Here are a tipper on the 8ft 1in tractor chassis, and a 3-ton truck on the 11ft 10in wheelbase. Trivans were used mainly for municipal work; a fleet of 36 Perkins diesel powered refuse collectors were supplied to Rangoon in 1939. As late as 1954 St. Cuthbert's Cooperative Association of Edinburgh converted 40 Mechanical Horses to 2 ton load carriers, replacing the petrol engines by Perkins or Standard diesels, and using Bedford rear axles.

Opposite page: The Scarab was a great improvement over the MH3 and MH6, having a lower centre of gravity thanks to its engine mounted behind the cab. These two are engaged on waste paper collection. Note the single central headlamp and horse's head below it. The Scarab name was a contraction of Scammell Arab, (thoroughbred horse) though the resemblance of the new bonnet to a beetle's back must have made many people think of the Egyptian sacred beetle.

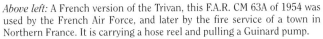

Above left: A French version of the Trivan, this F.A.R. CM 63A of 1954 was used by the French Air Force, and later by the fire service of a town in Northern France. It is carrying a hose reel and pulling a Guinard pump.

Above right: The only Mechanical Horse built under licence abroad was the French F.A.R., made by a subsidiary of Chenard-Walcker at Gennevilliers, Seine, from 1937 to 1970. From the mid 1950s they had completely different cabs of their own design. This 1952 fire engine with 24m. ladder has the familiar grille and nose, but a wider cab than Scammell ever used. The twin headlamps are also a non-Scammell feature; not until the later Scarabs did any Watford-built Mechanical Horse have more than one lamp.

Left: Among the many differences between the MH series and the Scarab, the position of the engine and gearbox necessitated a radiator immediately behind the cab. The air supply for this was via a grille behind the offside door. Other differences included a lower angle for the steering column and re-location of the fuel tank from the dashboard to the side of the chassis.

Below: Scarabs were exported widely, many going to Africa for municipal work, and as here, for brewery transport. The side-mounted radiator grille can be clearly seen on this 1952 Scarab.

Above: Another export Scarab, this time a 6 tonner with a very long, low-loading trailer, in Malta. The boxes are labelled HQ NAAFI, Tripoli, being presumably supplies from Malta for British troops in the Libyan capital. An earlier MH3 or MH6 lurks in the background. Scarabs were also sold in Scandinavia, Spain, Iran, Egypt, Ceylon (now Sri Lanka), and Australia,

Left: Like the MH3 and MH6, the Scarab was used as a load carrier, again mostly for municipal work. These 6 cu. yd refuse collectors were supplied to Northampton Corporation in about 1959.

Left: A specialised Scarab was this recovery vehicle with Harvey Frost crane, it is one of two examples supplied for work in the Dartford Tunnel in 1963.

Above: The last in the long line of mechanical horses was the Townsman, with fibreglass cab, hydraulic brakes and twin headlamps. This was the first Townsman in general service, one of two delivered to a Bolton firm in the Spring of 1965 for distributing provisions to schools, shops and canteens.

Below left: The Scarab Four was a hybrid vehicle combining the cab and independent front suspension of the Standard Atlas van, with the Scarab rear end. Although the cab was that of the Atlas (later re-named Leyland 15 or 20), the floor was unobstructed because of the location of the engine. This trailer for cosmetics manufacturer Coty has a higher than usual loading height, as it was designed to suit fork-lift loading of palletized goods. *Below:* Scarab Four chassis.

CHAPTER SIX

The Rigid Eight

The rigid eight wheeler was a peculiarly British type of truck, although it has been widely used by Continental manufacturers since the 1970s. It arose from the regulations of the Road Traffic Act of 1930, which allowed a gross vehicle weight of 19 tons on three axles and 22 tons on four. As an extra axle accounted for about one ton of additional weight, and the payload could be increased by two to three tons, the eight wheeler made sense to operators. Manufacturers who already made six wheelers, such as Sentinel, A.E.C. and Leyland, could produce a rigid eight with little difficulty, but Scammell only made a bonnetted six, and a bonnetted eight wheeler would have been wasteful of space. In order to enter the market Scammell had to come up with a completely fresh design, but it was clearly an important market to enter, as by 1936 nearly all Britain's heavy truck makers were building rigid eights.

Tested in 1936 and in production from April 1937, the Scammell Rigid Eight used the familiar 7-litre petrol engine to start with, but the more powerful Gardner 6LW was soon adopted. A 17ft 5in wheelbase and a compact cab allowed for 25ft 6in of body space. Transmission was by Scammell's six-speed gearbox to a bevel-driven differential and epicyclic secondary reduction gears on the leading rear axle. This gave an efficiency of 92.5% on bottom gear, compared with as little as 81% from some competitors with worm drive. Rear suspension was by Scammell's familiar rubber blocks when single wheels were used, and steel springs with twins. The front wheels were also rubber

suspended, with load-equalising bogies running on stub axles which were swivel-pinned to the main axles.

The Scammell Rigid Eight was lighter than most of its competitors, thanks to ingenious designs such as channel pressings instead of forgings for pedals and handlevers. Some comparative figures, from Commercial Motor Road Tests, are as follows:

	Scammell		AEC Mammoth Major		Armstrong-Saurer Samson	
	Tons	Cwt	Tons	Cwt	Tons	Cwt
Chassis	5	15½	6	13½	6	1
Body		19½	1	2		18
Payload	15	0	14	3¼	14	15
Observer and driver		2½		2½		2½
Equipment		2½		5		3½
Total	22	0	22	6¼	22	0

Fuel consumption figures, not absolutely comparable as different routes were used, were 12.18 mpg for the Gardner-powered Scammell, 7.25 mpg for the AEC, and 9.20 mpg for the Armstrong-Saurer.

Below: The first two production Rigid Eights are seen in this line-up of Scammells operated by G.Pickin & Sons of Rotherham, Yorkshire. Taken in the spring of 1937 the photo shows all of Pickin's Scammell fleet including three Mechanical Horses and four elderly Rigid Sixes. Pickin's business started in 1850 with a single horse and cart when the Sheffield to Rotherham railway was being built. By the First World War they had 115 horse-drawn vehicles on local contract work, later turning to steam and then petrol lorries. They were the first hauliers in the district to use the Mechanical Horse. Nationalised in 1949, some of their fleet was acquired by S Harrison & Sons, Sheffield, on denationalisation in 1954, including these two Rigid Eights.

Left: By 1938 the Rigid Eight had acquired a more modern cab, with front-hinged doors, deeper windscreen and radiator flush with the cab front. This remained unchanged until the coming of the Routeman in 1960. ET 9957 shown here was one of Pickin's original eight wheelers acquired by Harrisons in 1954 and fitted with a new cab from Scammell in 1956. It and ET 9958, similarly recabbed, were used until about 1965, and are still in Harrison's ownership. It has the single rear wheels which used the Scammell patent suspension developed for the bonnetted rigid sixes. Eights with twin rear wheels had conventional semi elliptics. One of the regular jobs of Harrisons' Rigid Eights was taking iron forgings from Sheffield to the Vauxhall works at Luton.

By the outbreak of war, about 100 Rigid Eights had been made, and they were popular for long-distance trunking work with such firms as General Roadways and Fisher Renwick, as well as tanker operators. They reappeared on the market after the war, now with the option of 8x4 drive, and were made with remarkably little change until 1960. Meadows engines were an alternative to the Gardner, and results of the Scammell-Leyland merger included the option of an AEC-Thornycroft gearbox as well as Scammell's constant mesh six speeder. and an Albion non-reactive bogie.

The 1960 Earls Court Show saw a new eight wheeler, the Routeman Mark 1. This had a grp cab with wrap-around windscreen shared with the Handyman tractive unit. Engines in the Routeman were either Gardner or Leyland, and most were supplied with 8x2 drive, though there were a few 8x4s, and some 6x2s, as Scammell had no other rigid six chassis at that time. Less than 100 examples were made of the Routeman Mark 1, the first and last going to United Molasses.

In August 1962 the Routeman 1 gave way to the Mark 2 with its distinctive cab designed by Michelotti. His first British work was his styling of the Triumph Herald, and when Leyland acquired Standard-Triumph in 1961 he was brought into their orbit. The new fibreglass cab was very striking, but a drawback was that it was non tilting. The Leyland group did not have a tilt cab available until the Ergomatic cab of 1965, which interestingly, Scammell never used. The Routeman 2 was designed to operate up to the new gross weight of 24 tons, permitted since 1954, and was engineered for operation up to 28 tons, which would come into operation in 1964.

Despite its very different appearance, the Mark 2 was generally similar to the Mark 1, with the same engine options of Leyland O.600 or O.680, or Gardner 6LW or 6LX. The gearbox was the Scammell six-speed constant mesh, and drive was normally to the leading rear axle, though 8x4 was available from 1968. The Mark 3, made from 1969 to 1980 had rectangular headlamps but was otherwise similar to the Mark 2. The Rolls-Royce Eagle was a later engine option as was the Leyland TL11 from 1979.

Like other British manufacturers, Scammell benefited from an upturn in rigid eight sales resulting from legislation in 1972 allowing 30 tons GVW. The Routeman models were widely used as tankers, both for fuel and industrial liquids, and also as tippers for sand and gravel carrying. A major customer for the latter work was Amey Roadstone. A number were used by the Forestry Commission, fitted with a HIAB crane. In 1980 the three eight-wheelers within the Leyland Group - AEC Mammoth Major, Leyland Octopus and Scammell Routeman- were replaced by a single model. This used the Leyland T45 cab styled by Ogle Design Ltd and made by Motor Panels, and was badged as a Leyland Constructor, though assembled at Watford and badged as a Scammell S26 on export markets. Three models were made, the 30.19 powered by a Gardner 6LXCT, the 30.21 powered by a Leyland TL11A, and the 30.25, powered by a Cummins LT-10 250. All were six-cylinder turbocharged diesels. Transmission was by a Spicer five-speed constant-mesh gearbox, and drive was to both rear axles.

One of the most important applications of the new eight wheeler, and one in which the Scammell name was used, was tendering to the Army contract for the loading system known as DROPS (Demountable Rack Offloading and Pick up System) This involved flat racks for carrying

ammunition and other equipment, which could be unloaded from the truck to ground level, or onto a drawbar trailer by hydraulic arm behind the cab, driven by a PTO from the engine. A similar system is used for demounting large rubbish skips. Two types were specified by the Army, the Medium Mobility (MM) mainly for well-surfaced roads but with some cross-country mobility, and the Improved Medium Mobility (IMM) for more difficult terrain. Scammell were in competition with Foden for the contracts, both offering 8x6 chassis.

The IMM contract for 400 vehicles went to the Sandbach factory. Scammell did better with the MM, for which they secured an order for 2500, to be delivered between 1989 and 1993. Before production could start the Watford factory was closed (in May 1988); though rights to several models were acquired by Unipower (see Chapter Eleven) the DROPS contract remained with Leyland-Daf. Production was suspended when Leyland-Daf went under, but was restarted after an interval by Leyland Trucks. By the time the manufacture ceased towards the end of 1995 some 1650 units had been built. The original British Army order for 1522 was extended by small repeat orders, some of which were to replace operational losses sustained in Bosnia. Leyland Trucks supported the UN Malay operations in the hopes that an order might materialise from them. In the event the Malays ordered the Multilift Mark IV load

handling systems used with DROPS but installed them on less costly Rumanian trucks. Of the final total, 24 DROPS vehicles were fitted with side loading Rail Transfer Equipment (RTE) to lift flatracks directly from railway trucks and place them ready for DROPS transfer.

Below: A Rigid Eight box van dating from 1947, originally operated by Fisher Renwick, but seen here in B.R.S. livery when photographed in about 1955. Major Renwick was a director of Scammells for a while, having met Colonel Scammell during their Army service. Fisher Renwick ran more Rigid Eights than any other operator. Their high-roof box vans were known as Showboats and were in regular service on the London-Manchester-Scotland services. This is not a high-roof type but a lower height version adopted by B.R.S., high-roof examples tending to suffer damage due to the inexperience of some drivers. Note the sliding door.

Above: A 1946 registered Rigid Eight with twin rear wheels in the service of a showman. The double row of chromed front bumpers was not used by all hauliers, though they undoubtedly give an air of distinction to an already handsome vehicle.

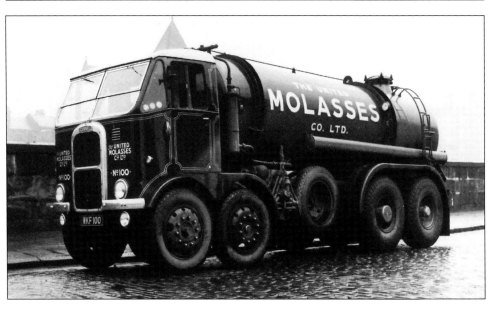

Left and below left: Tankers were among the most popular bodies on the Rigid Eight chassis. The upper view is of an early post-war model on a long wheelbase, so the tank capacity is probably 3000 gallons. The United Molasses tanker dates from 1958, and similar ones were delivered to this company from 1949. On the shorter wheelbase, it has a 2100 gallon tank with a three-cylinder air compressor seen just ahead of the spare wheel, for discharging the heavy viscous liquid. Giving 60 lb/sq in, the compressor was an O.D. North design dating back to the 1920s.

Above: A result of the Leyland takeover was that Scammells received model names. The Rigid Eight became the Routeman in 1960 when this new design went into production. It had a new cab shared with the Handyman tractor, Gardner or Leyland diesel engines and 8x2 or 8x4 drive. In fact, very few 8x4s were made. The double drive bogie was bought out, from Kirkstall, and necessitated a new gearbox from David Brown. The Scammell six-speed box gave a reverse direction at the output flange, which was corrected by the Scammell axle, but it could not give a throughput for a second axle. Four toothed sprockets and a pair of chains could be supplied with 8x2s to convert them to double drive for emergency conditions such as snow. There was a case in Central Africa where a user decided a double drive would be helpful, so he changed the rear end but not the gearbox. It drove backwards in six speeds and forwards in one! Two wheelbases were offered and six or eight wheel brakes.

Below: As with the earlier eight wheelers, the Routeman was a popular base for tanker bodies. The fuel oil tank on this example, operated by General Refractories of Sheffield has a capacity of 4000 gallons. The four headlamps were not seen on most Mark 1 Routeman, but Scammell was always ready to cater to customers' preferences.

Left: In 1961 a modified cab was adopted for both Routeman and Handyman. This fuel tanker was the first of five to be acquired by George Ewer & Co Ltd of Stamford Hill, London. They were primarily coach operators, though they also had a long-standing haulage department. The tankers ran in Ewer livery of Grey - Green, though they were operated on contract to an oil company.

Below: Another view of one of Ewer's fleet of Scammell Routeman that operated in Grey - Green livery. Interestingly, this vehicle is fitted with the earlier cab introduced in 1960 whilst 167 AUW, its sister vehicle, was equipped with a 1961 modified cab.

This page: In 1960 Scammell supplied seven eight-wheeled chassis to the Ministry of Transport for spreading grit or salt on motorways. They also had attachments for snowploughs. Powered by the Leyland O.680 engine, they had drive to six of the eight wheels, only the second axle of the front bogie being unpowered. A six-speed Scammell gearbox with two-speed auxiliary box gave twelve forward and two reverse speeds. All wheels were braked, by a dual system, each with its own reservoir. The reverse-angle windscreen prevented the accumulation of snow. The body and gritting equipment were by Atkinson Agricultural Appliances Ltd of Clitheroe, who also supplied similar bodies to Atkinson Lorries (no connection) for their 6x6 and 8x6 gritters. Douglas of Cheltenham also supplied a few gritters to the Ministry contract, but Atkinson made by far the largest number, about 400. Their gritters were closer to their standard chassis; the Scammell was largely a special job, and therefore more expensive.

Left and below left: The Routeman Mark 2, though totally different in appearance from its predecessors, was a logical extension of the principle of lightweight eight wheelers dating back to 1937. Designed to operate at 24 tons gross, it could carry a load of 17 tons, thanks to the low weight of its fibreglass cab and a suitable body. Chassis and cab weighed just under 6 tons. The cab, styled by the Italian studios of Giovanni Michelotti, used the largest possible one-piece mouldings. Power assisted steering, and braking on all axles were standard. The upper view shows the prototype, surrounded by Highwayman tankers.

Below: When the Routeman Mark 2 made its appearance in 1962, the rigid eight wheeler was at a low ebb in Britain. Impending regulations allowing 32 ton artics deprived the eight legger of most of its advantages, and it was relegated mainly to tipper work. This Routeman 2 refrigerated van of 1963 is, therefore, something of a rarity. The 1200 cu ft body is in fact, a lift-off container. It was built by Weston-Super-Mare Motors Ltd, with refrigeration equipment by Hydra-Lux. It was powered by a hydraulic motor driven by a pump from the Routeman's gearbox, but when the engine was not running it could be powered by an electric motor from a mains supply. This meant that refrigeration down to -20F could be maintained when the vehicle was parked or being unloaded.

Above: Like its predecessors, the Routeman Mark 2 was popular as a tanker. This one, bodied by Charles Roberts, was operated by drug manufacturer CIBA, and carried adhesives in bulk. Note the pump for discharge of the load.

Below: Chassis layout of the 17ft wheelbase 8x2 Routeman 2. Engine options were two Leylands, E.600 and R.680, and two Gardners, 6LX and 6LW. The specification included a detailed list of extras, with the additional weight they imposed. These varied from a rear towing member at 2 quarters 14 lbs (238 lbs) to a locked filler on the fuel tank, whose weight was described as 'negligible'.

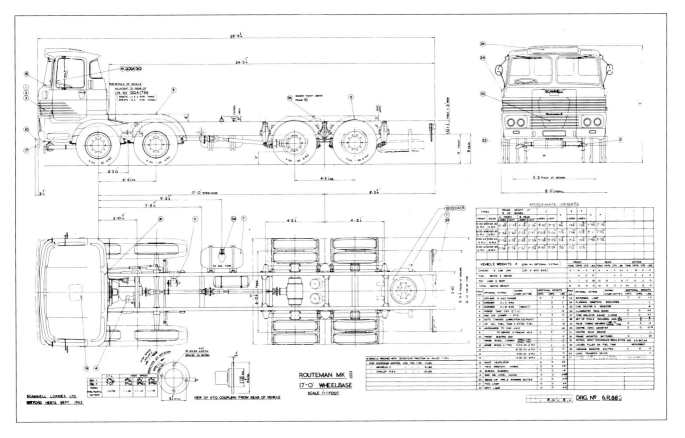

Above: This 24 ton GVW Routeman 2 tipper of Beedon Haulage carried the original Amey Group livery. Fitted with super-single rear tyres it is seen on demolition work in Swindon, removing the remnants of the former Great Western Railway hospital building.

Left: A Blue Circle bulk-blower Routeman 2 cement tanker photographed participating in the local 1977 Lorry Driver of the Year round held on the Longleat estate of Lord Bath, more celebrated for its lions than its lorries! The vehicle operated from the company's nearby Westbury works.

Right: Seen here 'week ending' in a Swindon car park, this Routeman 2 mixer began its life as an eight wheel tipper for Hills of Swindon Ltd., fleet number 324. Now lined out in the colours of Mixconcrete, the vehicle was on contract to that company being operated by owner/driver E. Gillett.

Below: A Routeman 2 operated in New Zealand as a livestock carrier with drawbar trailer. Powered by a 200 bhp Leyland 680 engine and using a six-speed Scammell gearbox, it incorporated a number of extras, spot lamp, fog lamp, twin-tone horns and a rev counter.

Left: United Molasses tradition of using Scammell motive power continued with the introduction of the Routeman 2, this example with its 2600 gallon Thompson tank entering their fleet in 1965. The company, however, transferred its allegiance to the products of other manufacturers after this model and Scammells were not to feature in its fleet again until examples of the Watford-built Constructor 8 began appearing in the early 1980s. Note that the registration number coincides with the fleet number, a tradition carried on by the company at the time.

Below: ARC's Scammell Routeman 3 tipper, fleet no. 4283, is seen in their depot in Chipping Sodbury on a Sunday morning in 1977, prior to going to work for the first time that Monday. Its newness was confirmed by the signwriter's chalk guide-lines still being in evidence on the vehicle.

Above and right: An increase of GVW to 30 tons in 1972 gave the eight-wheeler a new lease of life. Scammell's Routeman Mark 3 was distinguished externally by its rectangular headlamps, but more important were an increase in engine options to include the 260 bhp Rolls-Royce Eagle and standardisation on 8x4 drive which was an option from 1968. These Mark 3s, both dating from 1979, are a timber truck with HIAB crane, one of many operated by the Forestry Commission, and a bulk refuse truck with body by Lacre. The good service given to the Forestry Commission by the Routeman led them to order a number of its successor, the Leyland Constructor.

Above: An 8x6 S26 with DROPS handling system for the British Army. The system, which allows a load of up to 16 tons to be transferred to ground level by the action of a pivoting hook arm, was developed by Multilift Ltd of Shrewsbury, a member of the Finnish Partek Group. Loading/unloading time is 45 to 50 seconds. The Mark 4 hook system allows the carrier vehicle not only to lift the 20 x 8ft ISO flat racks, but to move them along the ground. The driver can reverse his truck, with the hook arm in its maximum down position, to the flat rack until contact is made with its A frame, and select 'lift.' They were delivered to the Royal Corps of Transport as well as the Territorial Army. In 1992 the RCT became part of the Royal Logistics Corps under the Options for Change programme. Delivery of DROPS trucks was interrupted in 1993 because of Leyland-Daf's financial problems. Total production numbers eventually amounted to 1650 units finishing in late 1995.

Left: A fully loaded pre-production 8x6 S26 DROPS vehicle awaiting its test driver's colleague at Watford. Note the Explorer, a reminder of an earlier military era, in the background.

Above: The Scammell name lives on. This smart Scammell S26 operated by owner/driver D.D. Paekau of Hamilton, New Zealand and running the colours of NZL Transport was photographed at the company's depot in Auckland in 1993. The current maximum gross combination weight allowed by New Zealand's Department of Transport is 44 tonnes, although only B-train combinations of a tandem-drive tractor and two trailers can currently operate at this weight.

Below: An S26 8x4 heavy recovery vehicle with equipment by Wreckers International, operated by the Lantern Group and based at South Mimms, Herts. The chassis was part of a cancelled export order completed before the closure of the Watford factory in 1988, and bodied later, hence the H registration which dates from August 1990/July 1991. Wreckers International went out of business in November 1990, and was acquired by the Lantern Group in April 1991.

Left opposite: Keveys Transport Limited operated the largest fleet of Scammell S26 eightwheelers in New Zealand during the late 1980s and early 1990s, at one time running fourteen examples of the type. Seven are illustrated here together with two S26 6x4 tractor units with temperature controlled trailers used for the delivery of fresh fruit and chilled products throughout the country's North Island. The eightwheelers, coupled to spaced three-axle drawbar trailers were used for the transport of glass, wines, spirits and beers. Overall length was 20 metres with the necessary power being provided by a Cummins NTE350 with Fuller RT115615 Roadranger 15-speed transmission. Three-stage Jacobs engine brakes were fitted as standard.

CHAPTER SEVEN

Dump Trucks

Despite the excellence of their products, the Scammell company found trading difficult in the mid 1950s. Military contracts were tailing off, because the forces were well-equipped with Explorers and other models made in the early post-war years, and with no major wars going on, they did not need replacing. The export market was less healthy, with American firms beginning to make serious inroads into Scammell's traditional field of the oil industry. Other specialist vehicle makers such as Albion, Crossley and Maudslay sought shelter under the wings of bigger firms, Leyland and

AEC, and it seemed sensible for Scammell to do the same.

In June 1955 they reached an agreement with Leyland whereby the Lancashire firm would acquire all the ordinary and preference shares of Scammell Lorries Ltd, a decision approved by more than 90% of shareholders. Scammell was to remain independent in design and manufacture, but could draw on Leyland's component suppliers, and also their dealer network. There was inevitably some coolness between the personnel of the two companies as Scammell men considered themselves the elite of the truck world and

Below: Three of Robert McAlpine's fleet of Mountaineers working on the site of the nuclear power station at Bradwell on Sea, Essex. Although many went for export, the Mountaineer dump truck was operated by other

construction firms in the UK, including Balfour Beatty and Costain. The Mountaineer's Meadows 6DC 630 direct-injection engine had square dimensions of 130 x 130 mm, and a capacity of 10.35 litres.

Above: A Mountaineer tipper of 1956, powered by a Rolls-Royce Eagle engine. Note the complicated routing of the exhaust, from a loop beside the bonnet to a vertical stack behind the cab.

were used to building more to special order. Mick Green remembers that one of the drawbacks of the new regime was that monthly meetings were normally held at Leyland; Watford to Lancashire and back in a day wasn't fun. Gradually, Leyland engines began to appear in such well-known Scammell models as the Highwayman. Another result of the merger was the appearance of new models, including a range of dump trucks.

The first Scammell dump truck preceded the Leyland era by several years. A scow-ended tipper with extension of the body over the cab was made on the short-wheelbase Mountaineer chassis from 1950. It had a 130 bhp 10.35-litre Meadows engine driving all four wheels, a six-speed gearbox and power-assisted steering. GVW was 18 tons, high for a two-axle truck and especially one with a wheelbase of only 14ft. The load accounted for 12 tons. The first were supplied to the Shell Petroleum Company for operation in Sarawak, but they later came onto the home market, being sold throughout the 1950s. Sales tailed off as site access roads improved with the use of bulldozers, and operators opted for 4x2 dumpers of greater capacity, such as the Aveling-Barford, Foden and Scammell Sherpa.

The first purpose-built dump truck chassis was the

Sherpa, a short wheelbase 4x2 with a half cab, powered by a Leyland O.680 engine. Introduced in 1959, it was joined two years later by a 6x4 on similar lines. Named the Himalayan, this used the same engine, bonnet and cab, with a longer wheelbase and rubber-bushed walking beam Pioneer type suspension for the rear wheels. Both of these trucks had a greater capacity than the 5 cu yd Mountaineer; the Sherpa's was 8/9 cu yds, later increased to 9/11 cu yds (22 tons GVW), while the Himalayan was rated for 12/14 cu yds (30 tons GVW). These weights precluded them from use on public roads, so they were strictly off-road dump trucks unlike the Mountaineer and smaller models from rivals such as Foden.

Dump trucks were phased out in the early 1970s, after about 125 Sherpas and 75 Himalayans had been made. A totally different model arrived six years later. This was the LD 55, a bonnetted 6x4 which started life as the AEC 690. Though developed by AEC, who had made various types of dump truck since the early 1950s, it was built by them only from 1964 to 1968, then by Thornycroft (1968-1971) which AEC had acquired in 1962. Both AEC and Thornycroft were now part of the Leyland empire, and when the Leyland Special Products Division was set up the dump truck was given to specialist manufacturers Aveling-Barford of Grantham. They made it under the name 690 Dumptruk from 1969 to 1976 when Leyland decided to reserve the

Grantham factory for really heavy dump trucks. As Scammell had inherited another Thornycroft design, the Nubian fire engine, they were allocated the 690 as well, which became the Scammell LD 55. Powered by a Leyland L12 engine, it was made until 1980. In the latter days of Scammell production, it was known as the LD 24, for 24 tons GVW.

Dump trucks needed to have a specialist distributor (Scammell had learnt the hard way, trying to sell the Mountaineer direct), and the AEC 690 was sold by Scottish Land Development. Sherpas and Himalayans were sold by R. Cripps of Nottingham, and when the 690 became the LD 55 both distributors claimed the model. Mick Green wanted it to go to SLD, but he was overruled, and Cripps were

chosen. UK sales were small, but quite a number found customers abroad, mostly in Ghana and Nigeria, but also some in Kenya. Leyland Ghana had an assembly plant which turned out 4x2 tractors and 6x4 trucks. A Nigerian company, A.J. Koreuni of Kano, replaced their fleet of 4x2 and 6x4 bonnetted AECs with LD 55s, and eventually had a fleet of 87 tractor units.

Above: The Sherpa was a compact machine with a wheelbase of only 9ft 6in, yet it could carry 8/9 cu yds with a GVW of 20 tons. This weight put it beyond the legal limit for public roads, but with an empty weight of 8 tons 8 cwt, it could carry a 7-ton load and still operate legally. The steel cab was made by Scammell, and the tipper body by Telehoist of Cheltenham. Tipping was by a Telehoist 'Telelever' LK8 double-acting gear with its own sub frame and served by a swash-plate pump capable of producing a 70° tip in under 16 seconds. Some Sherpas were supplied in component form to overseas operators.

Above: An unusual dump truck with 5 cu yd body on a Highwayman tractor chassis, dating from the late 1950s.

Left: Sherpas on the production line at Watford, with a line of Highwayman tractors in the background. The 44-gallon fuel tank was located behind the engine.

Left: Taking time off from dumping duties, this African-operated Sherpa is towing a low-loading trailer with bulldozer.

Below: A Sherpa being loaded by a RB at the face. It is one of a number of Scammell dump trucks that saw service with Hobbs at their Flax Bourton quarry during the Sixties. Such images now seem quaint when compared with the typical O&K hydraulic shovel and 170 ton payload Cat 789 combinations of today.

Left: Himalayan chassis at Tolpits Lane in the summer of 1964. It carries a test load, and the presence of a tradeplate indicates that it will be driven to Cheltenham to have its Telehoist body fitted. A few Himalayans had bodies by Edbro, and they were also the basis for mobile cranes.

Below: A complete Himalayan with substantial radiator bar to protect it from rock falls. The body floor and scow were of laminated construction, with a 1-in thickness of hardwood between a mild steel top plate and bottom plate of the same material. R. Cripps & Co Ltd of Lenton, Nottingham, were the sole UK concessionaires for all Scammell dump trucks.

Left and below: A Himalayan chassis with cab extended to full-width by a subcontractor. Other modifications to the dumper chassis included twin 11.00 x 20 tyres and a cut-away rear end of the frame to clear the neck of the semi trailer. The heavy-duty fifth wheel coupling was by R.A. Dyson of Liverpool who supplied the 25 ton capacity semi trailer against Scammell's order. There was also a Darlington Model 70 winch of 50,000 lbs capacity. It was supplied to Jardine Waugh for transporting plant and equipment such as bulldozers in Brunei. A similar unit, though with 30 ton two-axle trailer, was supplied to Amalgamated Tin Mines of Nigeria. A Sherpa chassis went to India where it was fitted with a locally-built cab and used with a 25 ton semi-trailer by the Central Water & Power Commission.

Left: The ancestor of Scammell's LD 55 dump truck was the AEC 690, powered by a 12.4-litre AEC engine. The same basic design was made in four different factories; by AEC (1964 to 1968), by Thornycroft (1968 to 1971) by Aveling-Barford as the 690 Dumptruk (1969 to 1976) and Scammell as the LD 55 (1975-1980). By the time it carried a Scammell name it had undergone slight modifications to the cab, though the reverse-slope windscreen was still used. Pillars were thinner, and the wipers were mounted below the screen. More importantly, a 202 bhp Leyland L12 engine had replaced the AEC. In 4x2 tractor version it was known as the Thornycroft or Scammell Bush Tractor.

CHAPTER EIGHT

The Later Artics, Highwayman, Handyman, Trunker and Crusader

Despite incursions into rigid eights and mechanical horses, the staple Watford product remained the bonnetted 4x2 motive unit descended from the original vehicle of 1920. The same basic design was made up to 1970, with steady improvements but no dramatic change. The most important innovation was the adoption of the Leyland 600 and 680 engines after the takeover in 1955, though the Gardner 6LX and 6LW were still available. Another result of the Leyland connection was that the motive unit received a name for the first time, becoming the Highwayman. Power steering was offered from 1961. A fibreglass cab with wrap-around windscreen was adopted as standard equipment, though a coachbuilt version with hardwood framing and metal and fibreglass panelling could be supplied. Export models used a thermally-insulated pressed steel cab. Some operators preferred to build their own cabs; Eastern Roadways did this because of their experience with bus body building. In 1958 Mickleover Transport of London NW10 produced a fibreglass cab which was specified by United Dairies for their Highwaymen.

The two-axle semi-trailers came with a choice of four suspensions, the familiar rubber-suspension bogie, a modified rubber version with four wheels independently mounted, an air suspension bogie, and semi-elliptic steel springs. These were the standard alternatives, but the catalogue pointed out that 'Scammell bogie semi-trailers are in most instances designed to suit the customer's individual requirements.' The frameless tanker was the most widespread type of trailer, and an enormous variety of liquids could be carried. These included beer, vermouth, milk, corn syrup, olive oil, invert sugar, sea water, fuel and lubricating oils, formaldehyde, carbolic acid, liquid latex, hydrochloric and nitric acid, molasses and liquified ethylene gas. The catalogue included an order form in which the customer could specify the viscosity and specific gravity of the liquid he wished to carry, with desired temperature and pressure. The liquified ethylene gas tank was insulated for temperatures down to −100°C, while for hot chocolate, a heated insulated tank maintained a temperature of +120°C. Other trailers included grain hoppers, tippers, box vans and low-loading machinery carriers. It is no exaggeration to say that there was no load or material up to around 45 tons which could not be carried by a Scammell semi-trailer. The normal GVW was 24 tons, but the machinery transporter was rated for a load of 25 tons, and considerably more could be carried in practice. Scammells were generally over engineered compared with their rivals, so that, where legislation permitted, they could safely carry or pull up to 100% more than they were specified for.

Left: This 'Artic Eight' motive unit was spotted at a quarry in Derbyshire during the Sixties. It dates from 1948 and had been adapted to operate as a ballast tractor for hauling a heavy duty low-loading independent trailer for heavy machinery.

Above: Until the Leyland era, post-war motive units were very similar to their pre-war ancestors. This 1954 example, operated by a well-known maker of mobile cranes, has the traditional coachbuilt cab and wings, and would have been powered by either a Gardner or Scammell-Meadows diesel engine. The low-loading trailer has the detachable rear wheels first seen in the late 1920s.

Though a successful and long-lived design, the bonnetted motive unit was not universally popular. Drivers found it basic and lacking in amenities, and the relatively long wheelbase compared with a forward-control tractor did not endear it to all operators. In 1960 Scammell announced their first forward-control motive unit, which they named the Handyman. The wheelbase was 8ft 6in compared with 10ft for the Highwayman, and BBC (bumper to back of cab) only 4ft 11in, so it could operate with a 27ft long semi-trailer and still be within the legal maximum of 35ft. The Handyman had a two-piece all-fibreglass cab with wrap-around windscreen. The standard engine was the familiar 161 bhp Leyland O.680, but as with the Highwayman, the less powerful 125 bhp O.600 could be specified, also the 112 bhp Gardner 6LW or 150 bhp 6LX. Despite the arrival of the Handyman, the Highwayman remained in production until 1968; after an 18 month interval, two more were made, the final one being laid down on February 11th 1970.

In 1965 the Handyman was redesigned with the Michelotti ribbed cab, and this was also used on a twin-steer 6x2 tractive unit, the Trunker 2. This followed the unusual 6x2 Trunker 1, with horizontal engine behind the cab, of which only three were made. The Trunker 2 was offered with the Leyland O.680 engine, now delivering 200 bhp, or the Gardner 6LX, and was built with the new 32 ton GCW weight limit in mind. Its most unusual feature was the suspension of the intermediate axle; a conventional semi-elliptic leaf spring on each side had an air bellows with pressure of 70 psi in the centre, between spring and

axle. When necessary, the driver could release air from the bags by a control from the cab, which acted as a load transfer of two tons to the driving axle.

The Trunker 2 went into production in 1966, a year after the Handyman 2, and both remained in the Scammell range until 1974. By then they had been joined by another tractive unit, the Crusader.

This was designed to a specification drawn up by Sales Director Peter Redfern for a modern intercontinental tractor with 300 bhp and 6x4 drive for GTW up to 40 tons. In the words of Edward Riddle, who had joined Scammell from A.E.C. in September 1967, "This was to be ready for the Earls Court Show in September 1968, and had to be very much of a one-man effort as the Design Office was understaffed and without a Cab Engineer or Electrical Engineer. I favoured a cranked frame to accommodate any V8 engine at the front, and a choice of wide tyres at the rear".

"Laurie Watts suggested a hinged radiator for frontal access to the engine in place of a tilt cab as it seemed unlikely that this could be included in our time schedule. It was obvious that an entirely new lightweight bogie would be required. I had ideas for this in mind before leaving AEC, based on coupled Albion bogies, which were not at that time recognised as capable of handling 40 tons. However my previous work on gear ratings indicated that this would in fact be perfectly practicable. I also favoured a new fully articulated bogie, basically of the cross country type. The whole rear end was quickly schemed up and passed to Thornycroft for detailing so as to avoid overloading our Design Office".

"The first prototype bogie was put together in the Spring of 1968 and fitted to a Routeman for testing; it immediately became standard Routeman equipment and remained so for the rest of that vehicle's long life. Thus the Crusader bogie was used on the Routeman before being seen on the vehicle for which it was designed. The Crusader did, in fact, meet the deadline of September 1968, and was well received in spite of rushed electrical and cab detail work."

Unfortunately the GM diesel was not popular for haulage work, though an excellent stationary and marine unit. One of the first Crusaders to be delivered went to Bass Charrington in the summer of 1970, and had an A.E.C. V8 engine. Another obstacle was that the 40 ton legislation was delayed and nobody could justify a 6x4 at 32 tons for on-road work. Peter Redfern got in touch with Walter Batstone, chief engineer of the National Freight Corporation with a proposal for a cut-down 4x2 Crusader with Rolls-Royce engine and Leyland heavy rear axle. This was immediately put in hand, and the majority of home market Crusaders were 4x2s. The 6x4 was exported widely, particularly to Africa and Australia, while another customer was the British Army. They used them in conjunction with two- or three-axle low loading trailers for carrying tracked vehicles, earth moving equipment etc. In 1977 they ordered 133 Crusader Recovery Vehicles with Swedish Eka equipment. They could tow a suspended vehicle of up to 16 tonnes GVW, or straight tow up to 30 tonnes. Most Army Crusaders were Leyland-badged, as were some civilian 6x4s.

Two developments of the Crusader were the uprated 6x4 tractor known as the Amazon and the four-axle Samson. The Amazon was built at the request of Wynns, who ran six between 1977 and 1985. Officially designated simply the 100-ton Crusader, they had Rolls-Royce 290 engines, a strengthened frame and lightweight Contractor rear bogie. The Samson was first exhibited in Pickfords livery at the 1970 Commercial Motor Show. It was based on the standard 13ft wheelbase 6x4 chassis with a second steering axle added. This eased the load on the drive axles and increased its potential. Powered by a 9.25-litre Detroit V8 engine developing 290bhp, and plated for 75 tons GTW, it entered service with Pickfords in April 1971, complete with matching Crane Fruehauf trailer.

The Samson was a fine vehicle but remained a one-off, largely because the standard 6x4 Crusader, although plated for 65 tons, could easily cope with more, so the extra capacity of the Samson was superfluous. It remained with Pickfords for nearly ten years, then passed to several other owners, and in the mid-eighties was employed on sub-contract work for Shamara Heavy Haulage in the Southampton area. Its job was assisting in the movement of up to 100 tons of cabling for Pirelli from Eastleigh to Southampton Docks. Today the Samson is being restored in Kent by Scammell enthusiast Roger Mortimer.

The Crusader was phased out in 1979, being replaced in the group line-up by the Leyland Marathon. First made by A.E.C., the Marathon took over the Crusader's production line at Watford. Some Leyland tractors with the Ogle cab were badged Scammell S26 into the 1980s, but the Crusader was the last genuine Scammell motive unit.

Below: An interim model of motive unit, this has the traditional cab and new wings with inset headlamps. The trailer is a 1040 cu ft hopper for carrying tripolyphosphate and sodium perborate. The load was fluidised and discharged through the bottom outlet with air pressure assistance. The unit was operated by Lever Brothers, famous as the makers of Persil, and could be seen in action in the demonstration park at the 1956 Earls Court Show.

Above: Another Lever Brothers vehicle, a three-compartment frameless tanker for powdery, granular or flocculent materials. A Fluidor air pressure system could discharge the load vertically to a height of 100 feet, and horizontally to 1000 feet. The 14 ton load could be discharged at the rate of one ton per minute. The tanker could be supplied with its own compressor, the familiar O.D. North 3-cylinder unit, or connected to an outside supply.

Left and below: Scammell were not entirely immune from the post-war vogue for streamlining, as these two photos show, but they were never sanctioned for production. In their 1949 catalogue it was stated "We have not pandered to the craze for streamlined fairings which, although they may present a pleasing appearance, are certain to reduce accessibility and to add difficulty to normal servicing, overhaul and repairs." The stylist of EOS 50 seems to have been inspired by the contemporary Leyland Comet. It is a mock-up with Scarab cab and bonnet, wings etc made up of wood, card and metal. The other is a 4330 US gallon tanker delivered to Shell in Cuba in 1953. It also has a Scarab cab, widened by eight inches. The wings, bonnet and radiator surround were made in the Scammell sheet metal workshops, but the bumper and chrome grille were bought in. It was a one-off, and drew the crowds at Earls Court.

MODERN CABS GIVE OLD FAITHFULS A NEW LEASE OF LIFE

One of the latest specialities of E. Wigglesworth and Co. (Stanningley) Ltd., Leeds, is renovating old Scammell heavy-duty tractive units. Very often this bodybuilder points out, such Scammels are particularly well maintained mechanically and they become old-fashioned in appearance before they are worn out. The Wigglesworth conversion therefore primarily consists of fitting a new coachbuilt cab. The cost of the conversion varies between £310 and £330 according to the customer's specification.

Before and after. These pictures show a Scammell before renovation and, later, after it has been fitted with a new Wigglesworth cab. The conversion takes between 14 and 21 days.

Above: An example of a replacement cab by an outside firm, dating from the early 1950s.

Four examples of the celebrated frameless tanker. Manbre & Garton ran a fleet of 28 Scammells in the late 1950s, supplying various industries with liquid sugar and glucose. They had a capacity of 2370 gallons. The Manchester Oil refinery tanker is at the company's depot at Trafford Park. The British Oxygen Company tanker carried 340,000 cubic feet of liquid oxygen. An annulus between the inner tank and its outer shell contained a special powder insulant to hold the temperature down to -297°F. This example has double tyres on tractor and trailer, but most frameless tankers ran on 14.00x20 singles, with smaller 8.25x20s on the front wheels. The Shell tanker for Istanbul, dating from February 1962, differs from the UK models in having a single axle trailer.

Above: A motive unit lettered to Joe Cross & Sons of Northwich, Cheshire, at Tolpits Lane in the late 1950s. The bow-fronted trailers were a Scammell feature from the 1920s, allowing maximum load space without restricting manoeuvrability. The trailers are resting on the pneumatically operated support legs which were part of the Heavy Duty Automatic Coupling Gear. They were extended by air pressure operated from the driver's cab. In the background can be seen another Highwayman motive unit, an export frameless tanker and, just visible behind the latter's cab, a Constructor.

Below and right: Two export Highwaymen, both in service in South Africa. The two-axle drawbar trailer behind the Kaplan for Coal semi-trailer gave an additional 10 tons of carrying capacity. South African assembled Scammells included some unusual machines, such as 6x4 buses on the Contractor chassis, and, in the 1980s, some S24s powered by turbocharged Mercedes-Benz V8 engines.

Above: A later Highwayman with fibreglass cab and wrap-around windscreen, coupled to a high-pressure gas trailer for the Distillers Company. The cylinders could withstand pressures up to 3000 p.s.i. They were carried in cradles at front and rear, the front cradle being rubber mounted to allow for flexing of the frame. The cylinders were retained in position in both cradles by spring-tensioned steel straps.

Left and above: Three examples of the Highwayman coupled to low-loading trailers. The Fitzpatrick unit is carrying a Turriff-owned Ruston-Bucyrus excavator and is parked across the North Circular Road from the famous Ace Cafe, gathering place for bikers who used to race from the cafe to the iron bridge over the old Great Central Railway at Neasden. The photo was taken from the large artificial mound created by the clearance of some of London's wartime debris. The other two illustrated both have the cycle-type wings which turned with the wheels, and were particularly favoured by Pickfords for their improved manoeuvrability compared with fixed wings. The company's Highwayman M2784, seen here in the evening light of a Summer's day in 1966 near Doncaster Station, had just delivered heavy components to the nearby plant works. The Highwayman was often chosen by heavy hauliers such as Pickfords, Wrekin Roadways and Wynns in preference to the forward-control Scammells right up to the model's demise in 1970.

Below: Gilbraith Tankers of Accrington were strong operators of Scammells, this late model Highwayman, fleet No. 131, was one of a batch of three that went into service with the company in 1966 to serve alongside its existing fleet of Handyman, Highwayman and Routeman models. The company continued to buy Scammells heavily for some years after this, but in 1974 Leyland Marathon and Buffalo models began to join the fleet in quantity.

Above: An unusual Highwayman is this 1966 model converted to a 6x2 by Brian Harrison of Sheffield hauliers S. Harrison & Sons Ltd. It is one of six that were still running in 1993 at 32 tons GCW. All are powered by the Gardner 180 engine in place of the original Gardner 150 or Leyland 680. They have a payload of 23.5 tons, and generally work within an 80 mile radius of Sheffield, though occasionally further afield. Harrisons have an enormous stock of Scammell spares, and hope to run the Highwaymen, together with some four wheelers, for many years to come.

Left and below left: The patent Scammell suspension bogie for four-axle semi-trailers, first used in 1933 and still current in the 1970s. Two sets of rubber discs in compression at each end of the beam took the place of semi-elliptic leaf springs, though these were available as options.

Above: The original fibreglass cab for the 24-ton GCW Handyman was an interim model, made in small numbers only. This one is coupled to a typical frameless tanker trailer.

Above: Second version of the interim cab, very similar to the first apart from the grille. The cab was built in two distinct sections, the upper part being removable to facilitate engine maintenance and even a complete change of engine. The lower part, below the floor line, incorporated steel framing, and was carried on four rubber mountings. Many components were shared with the Highwayman, including the Scammell six-speed overdrive gearbox, epicyclic rear axle, and front axle, but the gearbox was now in unit with the engine.

Right: A 'Handyman' Mk 1 in the livery of Accrington's Gilbraith Tankers. Introduced in 1960, the 4x2 swb forward control model was designed for use with maximum length semi-trailers. Seen here new in the early Sixties, the vehicle was to join a 27 strong fleet of tankers employed on the transportation of fuel oils, bitumen, creosote and napthalene.

377 BGO

Above: Introduced in 1965, the Handyman 2 used the all-fibreglass Michelotti cab first seen on the Routeman eight wheeler. The prototype cab was developed by the Malcolm Thomas Plastic Company and soon three Scammells used it, the Routeman 2, Handyman 2 and Trunker 2. Engine options were Leyland O.600, O.680, or Gardner 6LX.

Below: This Handyman 4 of Leonard J. Stamp is seen in their Avonmouth premises during 1977. The company, having broken with tradition at this stage by moving away from Scammell bonnetted tractors, still maintained the association with Gardners, this vehicle being powered by the 180-6LXB engine. The tank was primarily used for edible oils.

Left: Announced in September 1960, the Trunker 1 was an ambitious 6x4 designed for the forthcoming 1964 Construction & Use Regulations which Scammell expected would permit 32-ton artics. To reduce noise and fumes in the cab, the engine was mounted behind it, with the gearbox ahead, driving to the Albion bogie by a shaft which passed under the engine. It was a complex system, but had several advantages; in addition to a better driving environment, the centre of gravity was lower as the Gardner 6HLX engine was a horizontal unit designed for buses, and engine accessibility was excellent. The double drive bogie, unusual in British artics at the time, allowed a higher loading than with a single drive. The LAD cab was widely used by Albion and Leyland, and also, with a different grille, by Dodge, but only three Scammells ever used it in forward-control mode. They were all coupled to trailers with air suspension. Two went to Shell and one to Scottish hauliers, McKelvie. Production did not happen because the Trunker 1 had a tendency to go straight on instead of around corners on greasy roads when laden! Also it would have been expensive to make.

Above: Five years after the advanced Trunker 1, the name was used again on a more conventional motive unit, the Trunker 2. This used Leyland O.680 or Gardner 6LX engines mounted vertically at the front of the frame, and a Michelotti cab similar to that on the 4x2 Handyman 2. The drive was a 6x2, with the leading rear axle steering, as on many trucks of the 1980s onwards.

With the exception of steering and track rod levers, the first and second axles were identical, though the air suspension of the second axle was unique. The Trunker 2 was particularly popular with tanker operators who did not like the very long axle spreads required on a 32 ton four axle vehicle. The butane tank was built for LP Gas by Old Park Engineering Ltd.

Left: Pictured in the 1970s, one of a number of Trunker 2 tankers operated by Co-op Dairies from their depot at Latton, near Cricklade, Wiltshire. Similar examples were also to be seen in United Dairies fleet colours, both companies long favouring the Scammell product for the movement of milk in bulk.

Right: Carrying the maximum legal payload within the restrictive UK weight and length limits in the late Sixties called for some shrewd engineering. Scammells solved the problem with the ultra short wheelbase Trunker 2 with its centre-lift second steer axle. Shell were the main customer but this example in Mobil livery was photographed at Scratchwood M1 Motorway Services when brand new in 1971.

Right lower: A Scammell Trunker 2 in an unusual guise. This Wynns tractor unit acquired in 1968 and given the fleet number 254, has been pressed into service on abnormal load work hauling this fabrication on a tri-axle low loader as opposed to its more mundane role of working in the company's twenty strong tanker fleet, where it was normally coupled to a twin axle stainless steel tank trailer. By the time that this photograph was taken, Wynns were part of United Transport which in itself was soon to be sold to the British Electric Traction Company Ltd.

Below: This Trunker 2 of R.W. Febry & Sons is shown in their Chipping Sodbury yard in 1969. Powered by a Leyland O.680 engine, it was coupled to a small diameter tank trailer used to haul acids out of Avonmouth. At the time the widely diversified Febry fleet exceeded one hundred vehicles in number and were a familiar sight on the roads and highways of the south and south west.

Above: Swindon Transport Services was the creation of the Lindsay brothers, Basil, Dudley and Rob. They were at their peak in the 1970s with a fleet of a dozen or so vehicles. JMR 413F was their first Scammell and pioneered the practice of Leyland 680 engined units coupled to Crane Fruehauf bulk trailers with Pilot tipping gear. The vehicle is shown tipped for maintenance in their Lydiard Millicent yard on a Sunday morning in 1972. Although not suited to sitework it was currently doing its share of hauling stone for infill on the M4 motorway which was being driven through the area at the time.

Left: The prototype 6x4 Crusader, as prepared for the 1968 Commercial Motor Show. It was powered by a Detroit Diesel 8V-71 two-stroke engine giving 290 bhp from 9.3 litres. Production models had a different grille and lettering; most export and military Crusaders were badged as Leylands.

Right: The Crusader was a conventional motive unit with non-tilting steel cab made by Motor Panels, and Rolls-Royce Eagle engines in normally-aspirated and turbocharged models. Standard gearbox was a 15-speed Fuller Roadranger. British Road Services acquired many examples of the type, it becoming the backbone of their trunking services in the 1970s. This example was engaged on continental haulage.

Right lower: This much modified Crusader operated by Chelmsford, Essex-based S.J. Beckwith Ltd., was photographed at the Estover Industrial Estate, Plymouth in the mid 1980s. Commencing life as a 4x2, it has been converted to a 6x2 by the addition of a non-driven third axle enabling it to operate at 38 tonne GCW. Other changes include a sleeper cab conversion, non-standard grille and front bumper, round headlamps and the addition of a sun visor which somewhat detracts from what is otherwise a smart looking vehicle.

Below: This Detroit Diesel powered 6x4 Crusader was one of three operated by British Coal - the other two being day-cabbed models. It was based at South Normanton near Alfreton, Derbyshire and was used for the movement of plant and ancillary equipment. The load on its King tri-axle trailer is a Caterpillar D8L bulldozer and the location is the A5 near Tamworth in 1986. The Crusader was later to pass into the ownership of National Plant & Transport.

Top left: Moving house - New Zealand style! Building removal specialists Saxton & Hinton's 6x4 Scammell Crusader prepares to haul this single storey timber frame building to a new location.

Middle Left: The 6x4 Crusader enjoyed good sales overseas, Australia being one place where the model found a ready market. The driver of this Leyland badged example, operated by Ansett Freight Express and fitted with an air-conditioned sleeper cab, long-range fuel tanks, the ubiquitous 'roo bar and other essentials needed to operate efficiently in the outback's environment appears to be adopting a timid approach to the crossing of the creek.

Left: An articulated version of the Crusader 6x4 in the fleet of Pickfords Heavy Haulage seen here setting out for Switzerland with a crated load in 1978. The mandatory French 'Convoi Exceptionnel' sign is already fixed for when it disembarks from the cross channel ferry.

Above and right: A 6x4 export Crusader with tanker trailer. It was part of an Mobil order for fourteen delivered to Portugal in 1973/74, Two of the batch are also pictured awaiting export from Southampton in 1973. Kayser radiator shutters and double skinned cab roofs were part of the specification, power being provided by a Detroit 8V-71N turbocharged V8 with a 15-speed Fuller RT0915 gearbox. Regrettably, by this time, Leyland badging was being applied to models destined for some of the overseas markets, although in this instance the Leyland name itself still remained well established in the country of destination.

Left: A two-man cabbed Scammell Crusader in service with the British Army in August 1989. The load of two 8.1 tonne Alvis 'Scorpion' FV101 Combat Reconnaissance Vehicles on the flat trailer taking the vehicle beyond its designated payload of 20 tonnes. Over 3,500 examples of the Scorpion had been built by the early 1990s, they also being exported to serve in the armies of countries such as Belgium, Brunei, Honduras, Malaysia, New Zealand, Oman, Philippines, Spain, Tanzania, Thailand and Venezuela. The link between the engineering skills of Watford and Coventry was to be permanently forged when Alvis were to acquire Scammell's designated successor Unipower in 1995.

Below left: A military Crusader, badged like most of their kind, as a Leyland, carrying a Lance vehicle of the West German Army. All army Crusaders used Rolls-Royce Eagle engines, which were giving 305 bhp by the mid 1970s. Two models were made for the Army, for 20- and 35-tonne loads. The former had a two-man cab and nine-speed Fuller gearbox, the latter a four-man cab and fifteen-speed gearbox. The 35-tonners generally had three-axle semi-trailers, and could carry medium-sized tracked vehicles. Numbers supplied to the Army were 106 20-tonners and 250 35 35-tonners, as well as 133 6x4 recovery vehicles.

Below: This smart looking Leyland badged Crusader is pictured here loaded with a Terex bulldozer in the white colouring of the United Nations. The outfit was en route to Marchwood, Hampshire in 1994 where the Terex was to be shipped out to the British Army's Royal Engineers serving with the U.N. forces in Bosnia.

Above: The 6x4 Crusader was operated by Pickfords, both as a drawbar tractor, or as an articulated unit, as illustrated on page 104. This example, fleet no. M9532 is pictured here hauling a load from Rolls-Royce, Derby, on a four axle Crane trailer. A similar load follows, being hauled by one of the company's MAN 38.320 heavy haulage tractors. At this time, Pickfords had over a dozen depots dotted around the country from Glasgow to Southampton, although their Derby depot itself had closed in 1977. There was also a depot in Holland where a fleet of Volvo F88 units and York platform trailers was based, operating under the Pickfords International banner.

Above right: A Leyland-badged pre-production example of the Scammell Crusader 6x4 recovery vehicle, the British Army ordering 133 examples in 1977. The vehicle's basic specification is similar to the crew-cabbed tractor unit with the main recovery equipment being by Eka, Sweden, and consisting of hydraulically operated earth anchors, main boom and winch. Suspend tow capacity of the unit is 16 tonne GVW; straight tow 30 tonnes GVW.

Right: It was not only the Army who were to use the Crusader 6x4 as a recovery tractor. This example, with Holmes 750 crane, was operated by Lex Tillotson from their Halesowen, West Midlands depot. It was photographed at Knutsford Services, on the M6 in 1983.

Opposite right: Based on the current Crusader 6x4
tractor, the uprated 100 ton model CR100 tractor
was unveiled at the giant French Expomat in May,
1978. Using a Rolls-Royce Eagle 305, Mark III, six-
cylinder engine with a Fuller RTO12515 15-speed
gearbox and with a rear bogie designed for 28.44
tonne king pin loadings, the new tractor was to be
available for the home, European and overseas
markets. Intended to combat the established
European tractors, the CR100 or Amazon was not
really a true contender in this critical area of the
heavy haulage market. Both its design and
particularly its fixed cab legislated against its widespread attraction for the industry. The European
manufacturers had established designs, with
comfortable, well appointed sleeper cabs. In the
event only a handful of 'Amazons' were built, six
entering the fleet of Wynns, of Newport, South
Wales. One of these is illustrated here, although by
this time that famous name had given way to the
logo and livery of United Heavy Haulage. The
location is the Lyndhurst road at Totton,
Southampton and the load is a 53 ton storage
vessel, 68 feet in length, en route to the Esso oil
refinery, Southampton Water in late July 1985,
one of contract of ten to be delivered. The bed and
running gear of the 6 axle extending, self tracking
trailer is from the Nicolas range. Later in that year
United were to merge with Econofreight, although
it is not believed the Amazon fleet made the final
transition to that company's blue and white livery.

Above: An unusual 6x4 Scammell Crusader ballast box conversion. It belonged to the Department
of the Environment (DOE) and is pictured at their works compound at RAF Akrotiri, Cyprus in
1990. It was used in conjunction with a two-axle drawbar low-loader for the conveyance of small
items of plant & equipment to the various Sovereign Base Areas (SBA) around the island.

Opposite left: This Scammell Crusader 6x4 artic loaded with a Hitachi Excavator and operated by earthmoving contractor F. Burgiss of Tepohe, New Zealand was photographed descending a steep grade on the Napier to Taupo highway in 1993. Power was provided by a Detroit 6V-71 diesel; photographer Adrian Cypher recalls that it sounded splendid.

Right: The heavy duty Amazon 6x4 was a relatively rare model designed for specialist heavy haulage operations with such companies as Wynns of Newport. An even rarer example was this custom-built heavy recovery machine delivered new to J & K Recovery of Toddington in July 1983. It has Dominator lifting gear by Wreckers International.

Left: This 100 tonne capacity Amazon badged CR100 is one of two operated by the Ministry of Defence and based at the Royal Artillery Sea Gunnery Range at Shoeburyness, Essex. It is pictured here at a rest stop on the A449 near Monmouth during its journey to the ranges at Castlemartin, Pembrokeshire. The load on its tri-axle Crane Fruehauf tank transporting trailer is a 47.2 tonne Centurion armoured recovery vehicle. It was about this time that the ARV model was being replaced in service with one based on the Chieftain's hull and mechanical specification.

Opposite right: Pickford's 8x4 Samson at 206 berth, Southampton Container terminal in June 1974, with its matching 60 ton capacity Crane Fruehauf tandem axle low loader. The load on this occasion was a 46-tonne package boiler being exported to the Middle East. The trailer's sixteen wheeled rear bogie featured hydraulic suspension and steering, having a manual override for very tight turns. The Samson was powered by a General Motors 8V-71N eight-cylinder two stroke, developing some 290 bhp with a Lipe Rollway twinplate clutch transmitting the torque to the drive axles through a Fuller RT0915, fifteen-speed, twin countershaft gearbox. The 'Samson' was based at Pickford's Sheffield depot and remained in their fleet for over 10 years spending much of its working life hauling loads to the European mainland and back.

Left: This Leyland badged eight wheeled Crusader, powered by a 6V-71 Detroit Diesel, began its working life in 1977 as a stock truck in New Zealand prior to being purchased by Linton Motors of Napier in 1982. It was used by that company for 15 years on general haulage, its Palfinger PK17000 having a lift capacity of 6 tonnes. Sold in January 1997, it continues in revenue work, now owned by an engineering company based in the country's South Island.

Left and opposite right: By the end of the 1960s, hauliers were encountering ever increasing problems with the king pin loading on tandem axle tractors. The use of 6x4 tractors with semi trailers had increased in leaps and bounds since the 1968 Transport Act, and its ramifications vibrated through the haulage industry. At the same time the day of the 4x2 draw-bar tractor with attendant trailer in heavy haulage was slowly drawing to its close. In 1970 Scammell unveiled a new tractor for Pickfords Heavy Haulage which was intended to address the king pin loading problem. This was the Samson, based on the existing 6x4 tractor, of four metre wheelbase, with a second steering axle. This second steering axle, fitted with both leaf spring and air suspension, effectively enabled Scammell to uprate the vehicle to 75 tonnes GTW. With the 6x4 models, the rear bogie had an imposed loading capacity of 22 tons, in the Samson this was raised to 27 tons. The fourth axle installation permitted the 5th. wheel coupling to be repositioned some 87cm. ahead of the rear drive bogie centre line. The chassis frame was reinforced with 2cm. thick tapered steel plates, giving a chassis depth of 45cm. beneath the rear 5th. wheel coupling. Each steering axle in the tractor was rated at 7 tons, whilst the tandem-drive rear bogie was rated at 23 tons. In order to accommodate the second steering axle on the Crusader chassis wheelbase, some equipment had to be repositioned and the Samson subsequently had twin 35 gallon fuel tanks mounted on the chassis behind the front axle. Overall it represented a step forward in British tractor design being relatively compact and flexible. If the concept had been developed, perhaps fitted with a Cummins power unit and utilising the later cab fitted to the S26 models, Scammell would have been well placed to meet the demand for a four axle tractor which arose after the overhaul of the Special Types Act. Sadly by the time this became effective, the sun was setting over Tolpits Lane, and it was left to imported makes to fill the gap in the market.

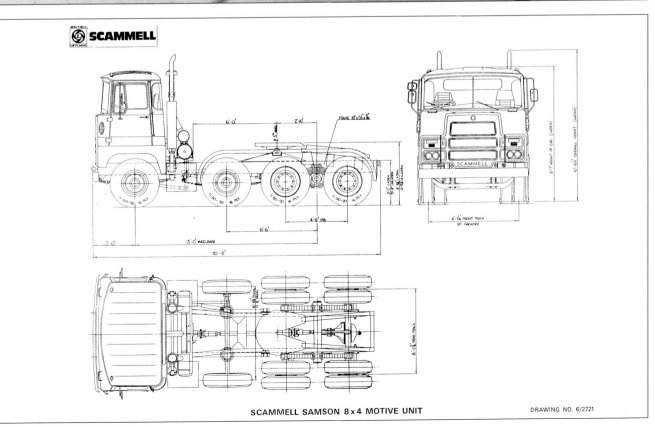

SCAMMELL SAMSON 8 x 4 MOTIVE UNIT

DRAWING NO. 6/2721

Above: The Samson, now in the livery of Shamara Heavy Haulage, fitted with a ballast box and featuring very heavy duty towing/pushing eyes fore and aft, is pictured assisting the Pirelli Cable Company's four axle draw-bar trailer in February 1985 as it rolls down the M27 towards Southampton.

Right: After the Samson was sold out of service by Pickfords in the early 1980s it was to turn up in the compound of Cranes & Commercials in Southampton docks. Eventually purchased by Tony Kimber and rebuilt in his North Baddesley workshops near Romsey, it re-emerged fitted with a stylish ballast body in the livery of Shamara Heavy Haulage. It soon entered service at the rear of the Pirelli Cable Company's four-axle draw-bar, which was used to transport underwater telephone cable in a large drum between the company's Eastleigh plant and its subsidiary Southampton location adjacent to the docks. The trailer, although of recent construction and modern design, did not feature trunnion type steering axles, and was very much a challenge to move in other than a straight line. Bearing in mind the modern technology available at the time this could be regarded as a step backwards, rather than forwards, in transport innovation. The location of this mid 1980s picture is Leigh Road, Eastleigh, Hants. After a number of years of being laid up, the Samson's future has been hopefully secured for it has recently been purchased by a Scammell enthusiast from Kent.

CHAPTER NINE

Heavy Haulage: Constructor, Contractor, Commander and S24

Ever since the days of the 100 tonner, Scammell had been used to providing transport for the heaviest loads that British industry might demand. By 1950 they saw this position being eroded; the Pioneer-derived 80 tonner was only a stop gap, derived from a twenty year old design, and the contract for the Army's tank transporter went to Thornycroft with their Mighty Antar, powered by an 18-litre V8 Rover Meteorite engine, and later, more effectively by a Rolls-Royce. There was a danger that Scammell might lose one of their best customers, the Iraq Petroleum Company, if they did not come up with a Pioneer replacement, and the answer was the Constructor, announced in 1952.

The Scammell Constructor was clearly a member of the Mountaineer/Explorer family, but with six wheels, all driven via three Scammell epicyclic axles and with the familiar six-speed gearbox supplemented by a two-speed auxiliary. The first 200 Constructors used the Meadows 6DC630 diesel engine, but then the 12.17-litre 185 bhp Rolls-Royce C6NFL was adopted. The cheaper Meadows unit could still be had on request. The cab was similar to that of the recently discontinued Bedford O-Series; Scammell worked closely with the Luton firm on the Bedford-Scammell articulated trucks, and when the rights to the O-Series cab became available, they quickly snapped them up. The pressings were the work of Willenhall Engineering, and the doors were made by Scammell. The same cab was used on the Mountaineer, and front

Below: A pre-production Constructor on test in 1951. Front and rear suspension were basically similar to those of the Pioneer.

Above: The Constructor used in The Commercial Motor road test in 1955. It is lettered to Sunter Bros, and delivery was delayed until the magazine had completed its six-day test. Like most Constructors operated by heavy haulage companies, it has a roomy coachbuilt cab instead of the Bedford-type of the original models. This was necessary to accommodate the several crew needed for work with difficult loads. The winch operator had his own rearward facing seat. A further five Constructors – two 'Supers' and three 'Juniors' – were to join the company's fleet during the next twelve years.

suspension was also shared with the 4x4 model. Rear suspension was by semi elliptics.

An example of the challenging work undertaken by Constructors was the transport in December 1956 by Pickfords of a 130-ton transformer made by C.A. Parsons of Newcastle-on-Tyne from Liverpool docks to a power station at Ferrybridge, Yorkshire. Because the roads on the 100 mile route from Newcastle to Ferrybridge were inadequate, the load had to be taken by sea around Scotland to Liverpool, and thence by road to Ferrybridge, a total journey of some 900 miles. Three Constructors with 185bhp Rolls-Royce engines were used, one hauling and two pushing. The trailer was a Crane with hydraulically suspended twelve-wheeled bogies at front and rear, and a capacity of 200 tons. The total train weight of trailer, load and the three tractors was 250 tons. The 90 mile run to Ferrybridge took six days. Pickfords' Constructors were frequently called on to transport Parsons transformers, some weighing up to 165 tons.

Two variations soon appeared; 1957 saw the Junior Constructor, similar in appearance but with a Leyland O.680 engine and a non-driven front axle, while in 1958 came the Super Constructor. This was again a 6x6 but in place of the Scammell gearbox it had an eight-speed semi-automatic unit by Self Changing Gears. There was no clutch or heavy gear lever, changing being effectuated by small steering-column mounted lever like that of a pre selector. The lever was moved progressively forward (left to right) to go up through the gears, and backwards to return to first. To obtain neutral, a knob at the top of the gear lever was depressed. The Super Constructor's engine was a 230 bhp 15.2-litre Leyland 900 six-cylinder diesel, though an even more powerful unit, the supercharged Rolls-Royce C6.S of 250 bhp could be fitted.

The Super Constructor was not as widely used in Britain as its smaller versions, though Pickfords acquired the model in batches from March 1960 onwards and Sunters of

Northallerton added two of the type to their fleet. In export markets, however, the Super continued to keep the Scammell flag flying; they were used in 6x6 rigid form for oilfield work, and with semi-trailers in Saudi Arabia, Abu Dhabi, South Africa and Australia.

Because of its excellent cross-country ability, the Super Constructor remained in production until April 1981, but on the home front it had been joined by a new model 17 years earlier. This was the Contractor, a 6x4 powered by the 12.17-litre Rolls-Royce engine, now called the Eagle and upped to 300 bhp. An alternative was the Cummins NT 335, the first time a foreign engine had been used in a Scammell. In fact it was foreign in origin rather than manufacture, for Cummins had operated a factory at Shotts, Lanarkshire, since 1956. Transmission was by a Fuller 15-speed gearbox, or the eight-speed Self Changing Gears RV30 used in the Super Constructor. The cab was a version of the LAD, though it looked quite different when headed by a long bonnet. All Pickfords' Contractors had four-door crew cabs with two-piece windscreens, closer in appearance to the Super Constructor's than the regular

Contractor cab. Contractors were rated at 125 or 240 tons GTW, the latter having larger hubs on the driving wheels and more massive tyres. As a tractor with ballast it weighed up to 50 tons, and with an appropriate trailer, 100 tons. This allowed for less than 100 tons payload. However, the GTWs were Scammell's own conservative figures, and payloads considerably in excess of 100 tons were frequently pulled. Pickfords and other heavy haulage firms often used two or three Contractors for loads over 300 tons or more. Their biggest job, undertaken in January 1983, was moving a 333 ton casting, part of a steel mill for Mexico, from Doncaster to Sheffield. They used two 240-ton Contractors pulling, and a MAN V10 tractor pushing a 24-axle Nicolas modular trailer. The outfit was 213 feet long and weighed a total of 533 tons. Other loads involving Contractors included boats of up to 150 tons weight, boilers, transformers, storage tanks and prefabricated frames for oil rigs, and what was in 1967 the world's largest mobile crane, with a capacity of 500 tons and more than 500 feet high. In the 1980s, Highland Fabricators of Ross-shire used two Contractors to pull loads of 1600 tonnes between them,

Below: For the road test, the Constructor was coupled to this 45-65-ton Crane eight-wheeled trailer. Working at a total tractor/trailer weight of just under 85 tons, with a payload of 45 tons, it recorded fuel consumption of 2.63 mpg at an average of 16.2 mph. The ballasted tractor alone returned 6.2 mpg at 26.4 mph. This was a busy time for Cranes as evidenced by the erection of the third bay to the 'new shop' in the background.

Above: A pair of Constructors with what was said, in January 1964, to be the largest payload trailer yet exported from Britain. The ten-axle Crane Fruehauf trailer had a capacity of 156 tons, and the overall length of motive units and trailer was about 150 feet. It was destined for Singapore's Public Utilities Board, where it was to be used mainly for carrying transformers and alternator parts from the harbour to a new power station.

although only on short-distance site work. The most powerful Contractor was the Mark 2 which was specially developed by Wynn's engineer Sam Anderson. He initially requested a tractor sans engine and transmission as he had his own ideas about these, but subsequently the new vehicle was made by Scammell with Anderson's suggestions. These involved a Cummins 450 engine and Allison gearbox and torque converter. Although normally used in pairs, a single Mark 2 could haul up to 450 tons, nearly double the rating for the 240 ton Mark 1 Contractor. Only six of these Mark 2s were made, four delivered to Wynns and two to Pickfords.

Although the Contractor was most familiar in British eyes as a ballasted tractor, some were used with semi-trailers by Wynns and others, while abroad they were widely used with semi-trailers and also as rigid 6x4 load carriers. In Australia some were modified by the local Leyland dealers to have four axles, resulting in a bonnetted rigid eight, a layout rarely encountered anywhere in the world. The first export Contractor went to South Africa, where they were widely used, including a number with bus bodywork for South African State Railways. Other export markets included India and the Soviet Union, who ordered three ballasted tractors and a 300 ton Crane-Fruehauf trailer for carrying transformers in Siberia.

A total of 1257 Contractors were made, the last being delivered in 1983. Only 73 were sold on the home market. Meanwhile Scammell had been developing an even larger

tractor, the Commander. Although it was shown to the public at the 1978 Motor Show, development work had been going on for ten years. In 1968 the Army called for a replacement for the twenty year old Thornycroft Mighty Antar tank transporter, and as Thornycroft was by then part of the Leyland group and concentrating on fire engines, it was natural that they should come to Scammell. The Contractor had never been adopted by the British Army as a tank transporter, as its 30 ton payload with semi-trailer was insufficient for the tanks generally in use. The Commander was specified to have a payload of 55 tonnes, that being the weight of a Chieftain tank. It was larger all round than the Contractor, with a cab height of 12ft 5in, width of 12ft 2in and a tractor length of 29ft 6in. (The comparative figures for the Contractor were 9ft 8in, 8ft 2in and 25ft 6in). The two 1978 prototypes used different engines, a 26.1-litre Rolls-Royce V12 giving 625 bhp, with turbocharging, intercooling and direct injection, and a 18.8-litre Cummins KTA 600, also a turbocharged and intercooled V12, giving 600 bhp. For production the Rolls-Royce was chosen, as this make was used in the Chieftain and Challenger tanks that the Commander was to carry.

The first order for Commanders did not come until 1982 when the British Army placed a contract for 125, to be divided between 7 Tank Transporter Regiment of the Royal Corps of Transport (BAOR), and 414 Tank Transporter unit in Great Britain. The domestically-based unit had only 22,

Above: A typical example of the work undertaken by Scammell Constructors in the 1950s. Pickford's PUC 472 is seen leading this move in December 1956, conveying a 130 ton transformer made by C.A Parsons of Newcastle-on-Tyne on a Crane 200-ton capacity trailer from Liverpool to Ferrybridge. Two more of the company's Constructors are providing support at the rear.

Below: Wimpey's Scammell Constructor and Crane 140 ton girder frame trailer carrying a machinery deck of an excavator photographed parked up for the night near Carlisle.

the others all being used in Germany or placed in strategic war reserve. The great majority were transporters for Chieftain or Challenger tanks with Crane-Fruehauf 62-tonne semi trailers, though three were used (in Germany) as ballasted tractors. Seventy were deployed to the Gulf in 1990, where they gave invaluable service carrying tanks and armoured fighting vehicles from the eastern Saudi port of Al Jubail to the battle areas.

The final Scammell heavy tractor was the S24, introduced in 1980. This was a strengthened version of the Leyland Landtrain, a bonnetted 6x4 (and 6x6 from 1982) made in rigid or tractor form, and intended for export as it was too wide for basic UK Construction and Use Regulations. The Landtrain itself was designed by Scammell but was slotted for production at the Guy factory at Wolverhampton, In fact it was made at Leyland's Scottish factory at Bathgate, with the Scammells and later Landtrains (from 1985) being made at Watford. As the Scammell S24 it was also made in 6x6 versions, and although too wide for general hauling, it was not debarred from 'Special Types' work, hence the appearance of a number of S24 ballasted tractors with operators such as George Curtis and Econofreight. The standard power unit for the S24 was a 14-litre Cummins NTE-350.

Left: Junior seems a curious adjective for this massive beast, but it is a Junior Constructor, the model which bridged the gap between the 4x4 Mountaineer and the 6x6 Constructor, having an undriven front axle and a Leyland 680 engine instead of the 185 bhp Rolls-Royce of its larger sister. It is one of twenty bought by Pickfords between November 1957 and January 1958. It differs from most Constructors in having conventional front wings, though this is not an infallible guide, as some Juniors had cycle wings.

Below: A typical Pickfords move of the 1960s. A long cylinder on Crane bogies hauled by a Scammell 6x4 Junior Constructor with a Highwayman pushing and steering at the rear. Note the minor damage to the front wing, for although they added to the aesthetics of the model - unlike the cycle wings they were prone to damage when manoeuvring.

Above: Most Constructors were bought by the major heavy haulage companies like Pickfords, Sunter and Siddle Cook, but this one was operated by Attwood Transport of London E.17. They were a relatively small firm, and this was probably their only Constructor. Attwoods are still in business, though no longer involved in heavy haulage.

Below: Edward Beck's Junior Constructor 'Katy' is seen here 'running light' with its Crane bogies southbound on the M1 near Luton in the early 70's. Purchased new by the company in 1967, it was later sold on to Chris Millers who operated it in articulated form before being finally exported to its third owner in Africa.

Above and left: Building contractors Marples Ridgeway used a Junior Constructor for work on the Hammersmith Flyover in west London in 1960. Working with several Crane eight-wheeled trailers, the tractor hauled a total of 204 beam segments (up to 60 tons each) which formed the main spine, 204 cantilever units (about 15 tons each) which supported the outer lanes of the roadway, and 408 road slabs. The total weight, which was hauled over about nine miles, was 14,000 tons. After this job the Junior Constructor was sold to Jack Hill of Botley, Hants, who used it well into the 1970s.

Top right: A more specialised military Constructor was this high-speed road surfacing vehicle which was built by MEXE for the British and US Armies. It carried 11 tons of grit and 700 gallons of high viscosity tar for road laying at speeds from 4 to 15 mph.

Middle right: A Constructor supplied to the British Army, and used mainly for towing 20-ton low-loading trailers. The large partitioned ballast box carried tools, equipment and ballast. There was provision for mounting an AAAA (All Arms Anti Aircraft) weapon.

Right: A familiar sight for travellers on the A35 coast road, west of Chideock in Dorset, is this ex Army Constructor in the livery of Frodsham Motors. Originally built as a fifth wheel tractor, it has seen a new lease of life in its civilian guise as a recovery vehicle. In the right background is 'Golden Cap', at 626 feet the highest point along the south coast.

Above: One of many exported Constructors was this logging unit for Spanish Guinea. The Dyson bogie formed a semi-trailer, and is seen here being carried for travelling to the site. With a 212 bhp engine, the vehicle had a capacity of 50 tons.

Left and right: For the UK market, the typical Constructor was a ballast tractor, but a number were used with semi trailers, especially for export, including this one on test at Bagshot, and a Super Constructor with King semi-trailers destined for Abu Dhabi.

Right: The front suspension clearly identifies this chassis as a Super Constructor which was introduced in 1958. In place of the centrally pivoted leaf spring which dated back to the late 1920s Pioneer, were two coil springs connected by\ a rocking beam. Note the exhaust pipe routed to discharge its gases behind the cab.

Middle right: A Constructor with the narrow, ex-Bedford cab, destined for the Government of Qatar in the Persian Gulf. The air-spaced roof canopy gave improved cooling. So far as is known, Qatar did not take any Scammells for its Army, unlike several other Middle Eastern states such as Jordan and Oman.

Above: Pickfords Sheffield-based Super Constructor 875 BGJ, was photographed in Oldham, Lancs, on a damp, and almost deserted, winter's morning early in 1967. The load on the Crane bogies was a marine diesel engine, assistance at the rear being provided by one of the company's Highwayman ballast-box tractors.

Left: No.160 in Sunter Brothers fleet was KVN 860E, Scammell Super Constructor, chassis No. 20897 with an unladen weight of 13 ton 14 cwt. and one of two of the type run by the Northallerton concern. It is seen here hauling one of the many ex-BR steam locomotives saved from the torch by the foresight of Dai Woodham of Barry. The locomotive, Southern Region Merchant Navy Pacific 35029 'Ellerman Lines', is being hauled on eight rows of Scheuerle running gear. Its final resting place was the National Railway Museum, York, where it is now displayed having been sectioned to show the internal construction.

Top: Quarry Industries Ltd of Plympton, South Australia, took delivery of this Super Constructor in 1964. Powered by a 15.2-litre Leyland 900 diesel, adapted from an industrial railcar engine, it had a curious trailer arrangement, a two axle semi-trailer to which was attached another three-axle semi-trailer.

Left: A number of Constructors were made in rigid 6x6 load-carrying form, including oil drilling vehicles and this fire engine, supplied to the Halliburton Drilling Co who were on contract to Shell in Venezuela. It had Pyrene equipment and two Rolls-Royce engines, one for motive power and the other for pumping. It could deliver 1800 gallons of foam per minute.

Above: One of many Constructors for the oil industry was this one for servicing wells up to 7500 feet deep. Fitted with Ideco-Woodfield servicing equipment, and an 89 foot telescopic Kwik-Lift mast, it was supplied to the Brunei Shell Petroleum Company in 1961.

Right: The Super Constructor was made up to 1981, as its six wheel drive gave it advantages in some conditions over its 6x4 successor, the Contractor. Later Constructors used another Bedford cab, the TL, identified by the dip in its window. This wrecker for the Dubai government is being tested prior to delivery, rescuing an LD 55 dump truck.

Left: A Super Constructor of 1973 for oil exploration in Indonesia. Equipment included a platform and gin poles for 30 ton skid-mounted loads, and an 80,000 lb capacity winch. It was powered by a 275 bhp turbocharged Rolls-Royce engine. Transmission was by the eight-speed semi-automatic gearbox.

Below: Just as they were major buyers of the Constructor in the 1950s, Pickfords placed considerable orders for the Contractor from April 1967 onwards. PGO 712E, fleet number M4945, was a 240 ton GTW example and part of a second batch delivered to the company in June/July 1967. It is seen here working with an eight-axle Crane trailer, the Hawker-Siddeley built load having gathered quite a lot of foliage on its journey.

Right and lower right: Two examples of Pickfords Contractors, both 125 tonners as indicated by the size of their rear wheels. SJD 803F has the standard wings while WYO 289H, one of a batch of eleven delivered in 1970, has cycle wings. Both have the four-door crew cab which characterised Pickfords' Contractors, though Siddle Cook had one of these as well. Pickfords disposed of their last two Contractors in April 1993, when they were sold to Indonesia, doing some work in Morocco on the way.

Below: Although operated by Derbyshire-based Heanor Haulage, this left-handed Contractor, fitted with a Cummins NH 350 and 15-speed Fuller gearbox, was not destined to be converted by them into an HHT. It was originally built in 1971 and supplied, fitted with a ballast body, to the civil engineering and construction company William Press who purchased it for use on a large contract they had been successful in obtaining in the Far East. On arrival in its country of destination it was refused entry for reasons now unknown and left to languish on the dockside for a number of months. The tractor was eventually returned to Scammell and subsequently purchased by Heanor's Peter Searson in 1973, it having travelled some 16,000 miles but had not yet turned a wheel in revenue earning service. Heanor removed the ballast body in their workshops and fitted a 5th wheel coupling, although they were to operate it in both articulated and ballasted form. It is pictured here, operating in the latter mode, hauling these 100ft steel bridge beams manufactured by the Butterly Company who were located near to the heavy haulage contractor's base. The front bogie was manufactured by Cranes, whereas the rear three axle self-steering bogie had its origins in an Atkinson tipper.

Above: Almost a mirror of the Constructor picture on page 124; Sunter's first Contractor is seen hauling here yet another of the many steam locomotives – Southern Region Merchant Navy class 4-6-2 35005 'Canadian Pacific' – away from that mecca of steam enthusiasts and preservationists on the South Wales coast, its destination being the Steamtown Railway Museum at Carnforth, Lancashire. The haulage of locomotives for preservation provided worthwhile income in the 1970s and 1980s for some companies but was no real substitute for the work disappearing through a decline in the country's heavy engineering output, ship building capacity and a decreasing construction and motorway programme. Following a rebuild in 1978, TYP 675H was re-registered YVN 308T.

Above left: Sparrows Crane Hire of Bath used this specifically designed Contractor to haul the base of their eight-axle 90 ton Gottwald mobile crane which had a maximum lift capacity of 500 tons. The Scammell's ballast box was designed to accept the crane's counterweight sections for use as ballast when towing. The vehicle was eventually exported to Sri Lanka.

Left: Although Wynns were not supporters of the Scammell marque at the very heavy end of the scale - the company's Pacifics & Diamond Ts providing their heavy move capability - the advent of the Contractor was to see twenty five examples of the model introduced into their fleet over the next seventeen years, commencing in 1965 with standard-cabbed versions, these being replacements for the now-ageing Diamond Ts. Two examples of the company's later 240-ton GTW models, 'Talisman' and 'Cavalier', fleet numbers 196 and 628 respectively, are pictured here, awaiting their next turn of duty.

Above: A.L.E. used their ex Wynns Contractor WNT 307S 'Intruder' to haul this 97 ton transformer to the new power plant at Sellafield. The location is Distington, Cumbria and GCS Johnson's Scania is seen following hauling A.L.E.'s Scheuerle trailer for the on-site transfer of the load.

Right: One of the first Contractors to go for export was this articulated low loader for Maitland, South Africa, delivered in the summer of 1964. It is carrying a Ruston-Bucyrus tracked shovel.

Right: Another South African Contractor was the basis for this country bus, with locally-built bodywork by Bus Bodies (S.A.). Five were delivered to South African Railways in 1966. They were the only rigid passenger carrying Scammells ever made.

Left opposite: Wrekin Roadways of Telford, Shropshire were late converts to the Contractor, buying their first in 1975. WNT 307S, acquired in 1979, is seen here hauling a transformer from the nearby Walthamstow works of Hawker Siddeley on a Crane girder trailer. This Contractor was later to pass on into the fleet of Wynns Heavy Haulage when these two companies merged in the early 1980s. It subsequently saw service with Abnormal Load Engineering – A.L.E., being pictured in that company's livery elsewhere on this page.

Above: Two Contractors with Dyson side-tipping semi-trailers carrying up to 50 tons of limestone. Six of these were operated by I.C.I. on private roads at their quarry and crushing complex at Tunstead, near Buxton, Derbyshire. They worked continuously for 16 hours a day, being loaded by mechanical shovels at about seven tons at a time. They were tipped automatically when alongside a parapet beside an underground crusher. The bodies rested in four cradles, those on the offside having massive outrigger arms which rested on the parapet. As tipping progressed, the body rolled to the alternative pivot cradles on the outriggers. A similar trailer pulled by a KV-cabbed E.R.F. can just be seen on the left.

Right: Contractors were supplied to many foreign armies, including those of Libya, Iraq, Kuwait, Jordan, Israel, Kenya and Australia. This is one of a batch with Cummins engines and 60-ton Crane-Fruehauf tank transporter trailers supplied to Jordan in 1971. They supplemented a fleet of Constructors with similar semi-trailers, delivered ten years before.

Right: A Contractor hauling iron ore in Groote Eyland, Australia. Each of the Australian-built Gitsham trailers carried 45 tons. The GTW was 120 tons. Bogie capacity of the tractor was 30 tons, and power came from a 335 bhp Cummins NTK 335 diesel.

Below: Originally exported to New Zealand in 1971, this Cummins 335 powered Contractor equipped with a 20-speed Spicer gearbox was operating with Hookers Heavy Haulage when photographed in 1993. In 1995 it was purchased by Rotorua Towing and converted into a wrecker being fitted with Holmes 600 recovery gear, a Garwood winch off a fishing trawler and under-reach gear by Mertec Engineering.

Above: Scammell never listed an 8x4 Contractor, but this one was assembled by Leyland of Australia in 1966 to meet the 4 ton front axle weight limit being enforced in Western Australia. Intended for iron ore operations, it was supplied to D.F. Rhodes Pty Ltd. With two full trailers it grossed at 128 tons, with a payload of 97 tons.

Left: Other Australian rigid eight Contractors were used for cattle transport. They were not conversions, but assembled from CKD parts.

Left: Scammell Contractors enjoying a second life overseas. An ex-Sunter Contractor is seen operating here in livery of Lift & Shift of India on a typical heavy transformer move using a girder frame trailer with Nicolas running gear. Another ex-Sunter provides assistance at the rear.

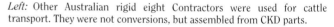

Right: A typical heavy haul movement for specialists Econofreight. Fronting the load is DBF 134Y, the last of six Mark 2 Contractors to be built, being powered by a Cummins 450 coupled to an Allison gearbox and torque converter. Plated at a conservative 240 tons GTW, the model was capable of running well in excess of this figure. It was originally purchased new with sister vehicle DBF 133Y by Wynns, passing into Econofreight ownership and livery in 1986. The sheeted load is a stator.

Right: Pickford's two Mark 2 Contractors – XUU 925T and XUU 919T – are pictured here heading-up the company's brand new Volvo F12 tractor on this 1:6 climb into Gateshead hauling 344 tonnes of generator inner core. Arguably, this 450 bhp Cummins-powered heavy haulage tractor was the most impressive of all the models produced by Scammell, although only six were built, the others going to Pickford's main rival, Wynns. They were rated at 240 ton GTW but their capabilities went well beyond the conservative factory figure with movements well in excess of 400 tonnes being recorded. Another view of this impressive operation appears in the colour section of this book. The Volvo, incidentally, was to last until the end of Pickfords Industrial in 1994 being purchased by Heanor's Peter Searson who collected it from Pickford's Glasgow depot, it having only done some 130,000 km with the company. He subsequently did not put it into service with Heanor Haulage but sold it abroad to the island of Trinidad, where it is today, working out of its base in Port of Spain.

Above: Pickford's Mark 2 Contractors in the setting sun climbing the bank on the Howden by-pass on Tyneside in November 1989 with a 220 ton rotor carried on the Crane girder frames newly converted to run on Nicolas bogies. The load is en route from Parsons factory on Shields Road to the Albert Edward Dock and onward shipment by sea.

Left: Ex-Pickfords Contractor XUU 919T photographed at the Moss Cafe on the A74 near Carlisle on 25th April 1993. It and its fellow Contractor XUU 925T were on their way to Southampton where they were to be shipped to Indonesia, stopping over in Morocco to do some work there. The Nicolas modular transporters were also being shipped abroad. Both Contractors were said to be in excellent mechanical shape; the only reason for their being sold abroad was that new regulations governing axle weights and vehicles width meant that they could only be used on site work.

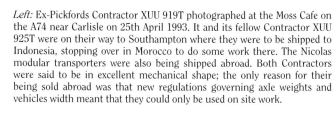

Left: This Watford-built example of the Leyland Landtrain began its working life in the Falkland Islands seeing service there as a dump truck on the construction of the Mount Pleasant Airport and other essential facilities following the short but violent war in 1982. On returning to this country it was purchased by Bowke Cranes of North Wales who had it fitted out as a recovery vehicle by Wreckers International with their MkIIC underlift system, this having a lift capability of 10 tonnes. In its towing mode the Landtrain was rated for 75 tonnes GTW. It is seen here in the livery of Auto Recovery Systems, Middlesborough who acquired the vehicle in 1992, although it has since been disposed of. It was powered by a 350 Cummins with a 9-speed Fuller gearbox.

Right: Announced in 1978, the Commander was the result of a ten year gestation, with valuable input from Thornycroft's design team, which had been merged with Scammell's in 1972. It had a Motor Panels cab accommodating four, with two full-size bunks. The specification called for a 55 tonne payload, but production models, made from 1983 to 1985, could carry 65 tonnes, this being the weight of the Challenger tank. A 20-ton Rotzler winch was operated hydraulically from a PTO. Minimum breaking load of the 26mm diameter winch rope was 40.1 tonnes.

Right: A Commander and Crane Fruehauf trailer carrying two armoured fighting vehicles during the Gulf War when some 70 Commanders were deployed in Saudi Arabia. They worked for more than 17 hours per day, using shift crews, with an average daily run of 170 miles. This hard work meant that they had to be refurbished some three to five years ahead of schedule. This took place at Unipower's Midlands factory.

Below: A newly refurbished Commander photographed at Bulford Camp near Amesbury, Wiltshire with a Crane Fruehauf trailer in the Summer of 1995. One of a number to be virtually written-off by fire or accident damage sustained during the Gulf War, it had recently returned to duty after being restored to its former glory by Unipower's skilled workforce.

Left and middle: Two rigid 6x4 S24s, operated by George Wimpey; a concrete mixer with equipment by Ritemixer, and a tipper working at 44 tonnes gross. Payload was up to 25 tonnes. At least two of these were ordered by the National Coal Board for off-road work. Transmissions were a 15-speed Fuller or Allison automatic with torque converter. When *Truck* magazine tested an automatic version they found that it did not transmit sufficient power to operate effectively on soft ground. They had nothing but praise for the rest of the truck, and felt that an S24 with manual transmission would be really impressive. Some 6x4 S24s were made for military work as heavy recovery vehicles, with Reynolds Boughton cranes.

Below: An S24 6x6 transporter with a 65 tonne capacity Crane semi-trailer loaded with a Mk1 Challenger main battle tank demonstrates its off-road capabilities. Developed from the civilian range of heavy duty trucks produced by Scammell, the Cummins NTE 350 powered prime mover was capable of 60 kph fully laden and had excellent climbing capabilities on poor terrain. The company also developed a similarly powered S26 6x4 tank transporter, for the movement of battle tanks on-highway.

Above: An S24 ballasted tractor with ten-axle Nicolas modular trailer, used by Mammoet Econofreight to move a NEI boiler from Rosyth to Mossmorran, Fife. The vehicle, rated for 300 tons GTW, was fitted with a turbocharged Cummins NTE 350 engine with a 10-speed Spicer gearbox coupled to a Brockhouse torque converter and began life with Scammell demonstrating its capabilities as a tank transporter to the Army.

Left: Econofreight were later to equip XTM 546X with this large accommodation/ballast body. Whilst no doubt it provides much improved facilities for the crew, it does little for the aesthetics of the vehicle. It was photographed en route to Southampton Docks with Nicolas axles where, along with one of the company's Titans, it was to travel abroad where the outfit was to be engaged in the movement of ship engines.

Left top: Whilst many ex-British operated Scammell tractor units have found a new life by being exported. Abnormal Load Engineering's Cummins-powered S24 6x6 tractor unit, rated at 250 tonnes and fitted with an Allison automatic gearbox and torque converter transmission, actually started life as a demonstration model oil field tractor, being imported by the heavy haulage operator back from the Middle East. The ballast box was built and fitted by A.L.E. staff.

Left above: In 1989 new axle loading regulations necessitated four axle heavy tractors. Many were converted by their operators, including the S24 operated by George Curtis of South Humberside. This S24, which Curtis has also operated as a ballast-box tractor, was used in the Falklands Islands in the construction of Mount Pleasant Airport during 1986.

Left: This hybrid 6x4 recovery unit began life as an experimental brake development vehicle. A close inspection of the Cummins-powered 'Iron Horse' reveals that it has a Contractor chassis, Crusader front axle, Himalayan hub reduction gears and a Leyland 'G' series cab - as featured on former Clydesdale and Reiver models. A longer fibreglass bonnet is also fitted along with custom-built steel front wings.

Above: Ward Bros (Plant Hire) Ltd of County Durham were one of the first to operate a Scammell S24 6x4 tractor, their example going into service with them in the early 1980s. The 120 ton capacity tractor, powered by a Cummins NTE 350 coupled to a Fuller RTX 14615 15-speed gearbox, features a sleeper box by Able-Body of Joplin, Missouri, USA. This addition, plus chrome exhaust stacks and a distinctive paint scheme gives the vehicle a pleasing transatlantic flavour. It is seen here in 1994 coupled to its 4-axle Transquip trailer transporting one of the company's Caterpillar D8L bulldozers along the A689 near Wolviston en route to an open cast mining site near Hartlepool.

Right: The George Dowse S24, pictured opposite, was purchased by Vehicle & Tail-lift Repairs (VTR) in June 1996 and subsequently re-cabbed by that company. It is seen here in its new livery at junction 12 of the M6 in January 1997 giving assistance, by way of a suspend tow, to the Scania owned by Howarth Bros of Oldham, Lancs.

CHAPTER TEN

Fire & Rescue

As we have seen, fire engines played a negligible part in Scammell's history, being confined to two examples made in the 1930s, some three wheelers and a few oilfield appliances on Constructor chassis. This changed in 1972 when they took over the fire engine building of Thornycroft whose Basingstoke factory was sold to transmission makers Eaton. The front engined 6x6 chassis were called Nubians, and Scammell retained this name, though they often carried neither Scammell nor Thornycroft badges, being badged by the makers of the fire equipment, such as Gloster-Saro or Pyrene Protector; later Chubb Protector. In 1977 they were given the names Leyland or Scammell Nubian, and the following year a completely new range of rear-engined chassis appeared, also called Nubian. These were designed by six ex-Thornycroft engineers who had been transferred to Watford.

The old front-engined models, with their relatively high cabs, were considered unsuitable for rapid intervention work with the ever larger aircraft which were coming into service. The noise from the engine interfered with radio communication between the crew and their base. Other manufacturers, such as Faun in Germany and Oshkosh and Walter in the United States, had gone over to the rear-engine layout, also adopted in Britain by Reynolds Boughton.

The new Nubian range was made in two versions, a 4x4 and a 6x6, both powered by rear-mounted Cummins engines in three models, the V903 (302 bhp) VT903 (400 bhp) or VTA903 (500 bhp). Allison five-speed automatic transmissions were used on all models. A Kirkstall auxiliary gearbox gave a further reduction of 1.98:1. When this was used in conjunction with first gear, the Nubian could be manoeuvred round an aircraft at no more than 4 mph, while still pumping at 3000 rpm. With the largest engine, top speed of the 28-ton vehicle was 70 mph. Tyres were 15.00x20 singles all round, smaller than on some rival designs, in order to keep the centre of gravity as low as possible and to make for easy cab entry. Ground clearance was not sacrificed, however, as the high reduction axles had small differential bowls.

Although intended for airfield work, the Nubians were built within Construction & Use Regulations dimensions so that they could be used on the road. This is important at some airports where it may be necessary to use public roads to gain access to a crashed aircraft. When they were announced the Nubians were said to be suitable as aircraft refuellers or general transport vehicles, but none was made in this form. They were designed in conjunction with the major top hamper manufacturers (bodybuilders) such as HCB-Angus, Pyrene, Gloster-Saro and Carmichael, and could be fitted with a Motor Panels cab. Most orders came from the top hamper makers, except for the R.A.F. who

Above: A Thornycroft/Scammell Nubian Major 6x6 Mk9 crash truck of the RAF Fire & Rescue Service stationed in Germany in the 1970s. After 15 years service these trucks were refurbished by Angloco. The model also saw service with the Royal Navy but after refurbishment were transferred to the RAF's inventory. The Cummins powered Mk9 was the first diesel engined fire vehicle to enter service, designated as Primary 1 crash trucks they remain the mainstay of the RAF Fire Service. Water capacity was 1250 gallons / foam 130 gallons.

Above: The smallest of the rear-engined Nubian chassis, this 4x4 carried a Motor Panels Mark IV cab and was powered by the 302 bhp Cummins V903 V8 engine. It had a top speed of at least 65 mph. The minimum cab height was just under 100in, enabling the Nubian to be carried in a military aircraft. Like all Nubians, it had a central driving position.

ordered their chassis direct from Scammell, placing a separate order for the top hamper.

About 200 rear-engined Nubians were made over a ten-year period, and they were supplied to many of the major airports around the world including Heathrow, Bournemouth, Birmingham, Newcastle, Dublin, Cork, New York, Amman (Jordan), Accra (Ghana), Belize (Central America) and Brunei. The R.A.F. took around 50 examples, and Malaysia, 25.

Scammell also supplied components to another fire tender maker, Reynolds Boughton of Winkleigh, Devon. Their Pathfinder 6x6 chassis used Contractor chassis frame, bogie drive axles and suspension and Constructor front drive axle and suspension. Mick Green remembers supplying well over 100 kits in the late 1970s/early 1980s. Although rivals to Scammell, Reynolds Boughton also collaborated with them; about 700 6x6 Constructors for overseas markets had R.B. recovery gear.

Left: Scammells were rare birds in the USA, but this is a 4x4 Nubian with top hamper by Federal Motors of Ocala, Florida. It was photographed at their works in 1987.

Below: A Scammell Nubian 4x4 Carmichael of the Royal Air Force Fire & Rescue Service pictured at RAF Coltishall in the late 1980s. It was a Mk10A crash vehicle, designated a Primary 2 truck. Water capacity was 600 gallons with 80 gallons of foam. The RAF's Mk10 series had a number of derivatives; 10A, 10B, 10C (Royal Navy), 10D (Unipower) and 10E, the last named being refurbished Mk10s. The original Mk10s carried 600 gallons of premix AFFF (Aqueous Film Forming Foam). All vehicles were similar except for minor cosmetic and fire equipment differences.

Above: One of the Scammell/Chubb Protector 4x4s in service at the Philip S.W. Goldson International Airport in Belize, Central America. They entered service in the early 1980s, being supplied by the Overseas Development Agency (ODA). The ladder on the side (American style) was adopted for a very short time. The British Defence Fire Services decal on the door was only attached for this photo, the RAF Fire Service (DFS) being located next to the airport fire station. Goldson International was also the base for the British forces, their side being known as Airport Camp.

Left: In 1994 a Gloster-Saro field engineer visited Belize to assess the Scammell/Chubb Protector 4x4s operated there. In this view another example is illustrated with its water/foam tanks removed for inspection. He was very impressed with the tidy state of the vehicles, they only being maintained by the fire crews themselves who had very limited engineering facilities in their station.

Above: A 6x6 Nubian Major with Motor Panels cab and equipment by HCB-Angus. Operated by the Irish Airports Authority, it was classed as an MFT (Major Foam Tender), and carried about 12,000 litres of water plus foam concentrate. A meter ensured the correct mixture of water to concentrate, which was delivered from the roof-mounted monitor at 10,000 gallons per minute. The range was about 200 feet, but at maximum delivery the water tank was exhausted in two minutes; auxiliary supplies from hydrants or storage tanks are usually available. The water spray ahead of the front wheels was a self-protection system, to counter radiant heat from a burning aircraft.

Left: The 6x6 Nubian Major, also seen here with a Motor Panels cab, used the larger Cummins engines of up to 15 litres and 500 bhp. The current Unipower appliances are on much the same lines, though the maximum engine output is now 710 bhp from a Detroit Diesel V8.

Right: A RAF Fire & Rescue Service Scammell Nubian Major 6x6 Mk11A crash truck with top hamper by Gloster-Saro. This vehicle is one of two in service at Mount Pleasant Airport, Falkland Islands, South Atlantic. The capacity of the MK11A is 1250 gallons water; 150 gallons foam.

Left: Believed to be the only 6x6 example to have been fitted with a US-built top hamper, this Scammell Nubian Major 6x6/Garsite was in service with the Port Authority of New York Fire Department. The fire department was manned by cross-trained police officers/firemen. The vehicle is now understood to be in the Middle East.

Right: A Scammell Nubian Major 6x6 Simon/Gloster-Saro Protector, one of two currently in service with the Norwich Airport Fire Service. This example, pictured here in the mid 1980s, carries 10,000 litres of water/1100 litres of foam. Its Godiva type GVA single stage centrifugal pumps provide an output of 5000 litres per minute at 3200 rpm. Laden weight of the vehicle is 26.9 tonnes with power being provided by an 8V-92TA Detroit Diesel developing 540 bhp at 2300 rpm through an Allison 5-speed automatic transmission. Note the painted hubs, a safety feature quickly identifying the vehicle in motion.

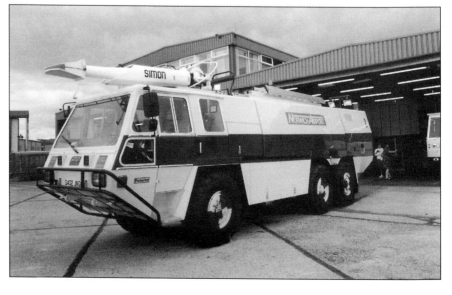

CHAPTER ELEVEN

An End
and
A Beginning

Up to 1980 Scammell was affected less by its membership of the Leyland Group than other firms such as AEC, Albion and Thornycroft. Though output was small Scammell was thought of as the flagship of the group, and was a favourite company of Donald Stokes, head of Leyland from 1962 to 1975. Unfortunately Leyland's involvement with cars led to starvation of funds to all the truck companies. In 1974, for example, the heavy divisions made a £43m profit, every penny of which went into propping up the car side of the business, leaving nothing for investment in new plant and models at Leyland, Bathgate or Watford.

From 1980 most Scammells used the Motor Panels T45 cab styled by Ogle Design which was thought of as a Leyland cab if only because there were many more Leyland-badged T45s around than Scammells. The 8x4 Leyland Constructor, which replaced the AEC Mammoth Major, Leyland Octopus and Scammell Routeman, was made at Watford but nearly always carried a Leyland badge. Similarly the 6x2 Roadtrain 38 tonne tractors had Leyland in large letters under the windscreen, and in smaller lettering below, 'Scammell Roadtrain 6x2'.

The S26 range, though also T45 cabbed, was a more distinctive Scammell product, using Rolls-Royce or Cummins engines, whereas Roadtrains and Constructors were Leyland-powered. In fact, although they looked completely different, the S26 heavy tractor and bonnetted S24 were quite similar under the skin. They had the same engine options and chassis design, though the S24 had a

Right: One of the contract for sixty 6x6 S26 self-loading dump trucks placed by the Ministry of Defence in 1984, the trucks being used by the Royal Engineers. Powered by Rolls-Royce Eagle Mark 3 engines, they had sleeper cabs and Atlas AK 4003C-6.2 hydraulic self-loading cranes. In addition to dump trucks, they could be used as carriers for seven NATO pallets or general cargo. During 1985 a further 51 were ordered by the MoD.

heavier frame, longer wheelbase and was 14.37in wider. Also Scammell-badged were 6x4 rigids and tractive units in the S26 series. Badging in Scammell's later days was very much a political matter. Donald Stokes favoured the make, but when his influence waned the Leyland name became more widely used, as on the 6x4 Crusaders. In the end Leyland's bad reputation was damaging Scammell's sales, so the name returned, on the later military Crusaders and, exclusively, on the S24 and S26.

In 1983 the Moor Park trailer factory (opened in 1941) was sold, ending more than sixty years of trailer building, not only for Scammell motive units, but for many other makes, in particular Bedford. The £2.5m realised from the sale paid for a new assembly hall at Tolpits Lane.

Scammell made 'small but respectable profits' in the early 1980s, according to managing director Vic Wilkes, although exact figures were bound up in Leyland's complex

Below: An S26 6x4 tractor with Crane-Fruehauf three-axle trailer, for a GTW of 38 tonnes. These 6x4s carried Scammell badges, while the 4x2 and twin-steer 6x2 tractors were badged as Leyland Roadtrains.

accounting. The Leyland link was very beneficial to Scammell, who could not have afforded to develop a new cab by themselves, yet they were still able to provide small runs of specialised vehicles. An example of this was the 6x4 aircraft refuelling tanker with S26 cab on 22.5in low profile tyres, enabling it not only to clear aircraft wings but to be carried in a Hercules when necessary. The cab suspension and springs could be clamped down to save vital inches during loading onto the aircraft. Fitted with Gloster-Saro equipment, 50 of these were supplied to a North African government in 1985. Some also went to the RAF.

Military contracts were very important to Scammell, and they profited from the Commander and DROPS work already mentioned, and also provided 6x6 self-loading dump trucks to the Royal Engineers. Exports were increasingly difficult, for more and more countries were turning to local assembly, and Leyland largely lost out on this. For instance, there were no Leyland equivalents of the big Mercedes-Benz and Scania operations in Brazil. In 1986 there were plans to sell 6x4 Scammell tractors in the United States; as neither the Leyland nor Scammell names were familiar to Americans, they carried the name Mountaineer on their T45 cabs. Six chassis/cab units were prepared for export, and later models were to be supplied in kit form and assembled at a small plant at White Sulphur Springs, Virginia. The difficulty of conforming to US regulations (12 volt electrics were mandatory, and Scammell's use of a 24 volt system was just one of the problems), and a fall in the value of the dollar put paid to the scheme.

During the late 1980s there were obvious signs that Leyland was concentrating its heavy truck making in the

Right: This left-hand drive S26 tractor featured on the Scammell stand at the 1982 Commercial Motor Show. Power was provided by a Cummins NTE 350 bhp., 6-cylinder engine with a Fuller RTX 11609A 11-speed gearbox. It was fitted with both a 5th. wheel coupling and a detachable ballast body and nominally rated for 100 tonne GCW for on-road operation. Although painted in Wynns livery, the finish differed from the normally darker red of that company. It is seen here in May 1983 alongside the Vosper-Thorneycroft works in Southampton's old docks, having moved a 72 tonne load of equipment from the Midlands on the 7-line Nicolas modular bogie. The S26 last visited the port in 1984, when still resplendent in the Wynns livery, it was exported to Kuwait.

North of England and Scotland, and after the merger with Daf in February 1987 the future of the Watford plant seemed very uncertain. The mergers coincided with the very important DROPS contract for 8x6 vehicles, and this went to Daf as a dowry. Although developed by Scammell personnel, the DROPS trucks were made by Leyland-Daf at Leyland with no benefit to Scammell at all. This continued until Leyland-Daf's own problems caused a halt in the Spring of 1993, as described in Chapter Six. A Scammell management buy-out failed and at the beginning of 1988 the workforce were resigned to looking for other employment.

'Enter Unipower'

It was then that the relatively little known name of Unipower appeared on the scene. Founded before the war as Universal Power Drives Ltd, they specialised in the conversion of four wheeled lorries to six wheelers, and in 1937 brought out the first Unipower, a 4x4 forestry tractor. This was made throughout the war as the result of a Government plan to boost home-grown timber production, and continued with little major change until 1968. Unipower then turned to a forward-control 4x4, the Perkins V8-powered Invader which was used for recovery work and later as an aircraft crash tender called the P44. This became an increasingly important part of Unipower's activities (their last 6x4 conversion was made in 1973), and continued after the company was acquired by AC Cars in 1977. Production moved from Chiswick to AC's factory at Thames Ditton, Surrey. Having expertise in the building of crash tenders must have been one reason why Unipower's Group Chairman Peter Rotheroe was attracted to Scammell, and why someone in the Rover Group suggested

Unipower as a possible saviour of the Scammell designs, though not, as it turned out, the name or the Tolpits Lane factory.

Production at Tolpits Lane ended in May 1988, (the last chassis, a Constructor 8, was laid down on 25th May) but a skeleton staff stayed on for final tidying up until the end of the year. In the same month Peter Rotheroe concluded the second stage of the purchase from the Rover Group of the licence to manufacture and supply spare parts for Scammell products. Spares were to be made for the Contractor, Explorer, Crusader, and Thornycroft Mighty Antar. The only designs which Unipower would continue to manufacture were the S24, Commander and Nubian. New premises were acquired on a modern industrial estate, the Watford Business Park, less than a mile from Tolpits Lane.

Below: Most Unipower 4x4 tractors were for forestry work. These three, numbered 189-191 in the Wynns fleet, were delivered in 1949, being based at Welshpool and Newport. They were powered by Gardner 4LW engines.

Above: An S24 (left) with its development, the C Series. This has a tidier front end with inset headlamps, and a wider cab with seating for a driver and either one or two crew members, and fitted with a fold-away bunk. A longer sleeper or crew cab could be fitted.

The managing director was Howard Barnes, former sales and marketing director for Scammell, and he set about building up a small workforce, almost entirely from ex-Scammell employees. Unipower could not afford to be too ambitious to start with, and the initial workforce was only 25, which had increased to 80 by the Spring of 1993. Scammell had employed 400 at the time of closure, down from 670 in 1985 and 850 in 1979. Today about 80% of Unipower employees, including secretarial staff, are ex-Scammell people. In 1993 the sales force was 100% ex-Scammell.

The first Unipower-built S24 was completed just before Christmas 1988. In the Scammell tradition, it was a specialised vehicle destined for the Llanwern Steel Works where it pulled 160 tonnes of scrap steel at a maximum speed of 4 mph on solid rubber tyres. It had only one forward and one reverse speed through an Allison automatic gearbox. Although another S24 was delivered

shortly afterwards, Unipower's main income to start with came from the supply of spare parts, to the Army and to civilian operators via the Leyland Daf Multipart organisation. Revenue from this business financed re-tooling and the modest production of trucks. 22 were turned out in 1989, 21 in 1990 and 24 in 1991. Orders received during 1993, 1994 and 1995 have totalled 209 units. They were a mixture of Commanders, S24, S Series fire engines and M Series military vehicles.

While the basic layout of these Unipowers (apart from the M Series) show their Scammell ancestry, many improvements have been made. The S24 cab, somewhat short on driver comforts, has given way to a wider cab, well insulated and air conditioned and with variable accommodation including sleeping space. This is called the C Series, into which category the other bonnetted truck, the Commander, falls. Other classifications are S Series for the crash tenders and M Series for the forward control 6x6 and 8x8 military vehicles. For a short time Unipower also offered the H Series of dump trucks which had been made by Haulamatic and Heathfield. This business has recently been sold off as it was not compatible with the rest of Unipower's activities. The dump trucks are now made by Heathfield Haulamatic of Burton-on-Trent.

As well as the Watford premises, Unipower had a larger factory at Dudley, West Midlands, where the dump trucks were made, though both factories were totally flexible, and in theory either factory could make any model. An example of this was that in the Spring of 1993 a batch of 17 crash tender chassis were being made at Dudley, and some at Watford. The Dudley factory was vacated in the Autumn of 1995.

The S Series crash tenders are made in four models, on generally the same lines as the Scammell Nubians, but with Detroit Diesel V8 engines rather than Cummins. Other modifications include a splayed frame to facilitate a lower and further forward engine location. The 4x4 SNN4-D and 6x6 SNM6-D both use a massive Detroit 8V92TA V8 engine of 12 litres capacity, giving 710 bhp. A smaller 585 bhp unit is

Left: This Cummins NTE-400-powered S24-derived Unipower was unusual for a heavy recovery vehicle in being a 4x2. Nevertheless its Unipower-built rear axle was one of the heaviest road-going axles available, rated up to 22,500 kg at 12 mph. It has successfully towed a Commander tank transporter, a 32-ton S Series crash tender and, seen here, a 30-tonne Volvo 8x4 bulk refuse truck. The front bumper was designed to accept ballast weights suspended below the bumper. Only one was made.

Opposite page: A Unipower M Series 8x8 Heavy Equipment Transporter demonstrates its capabilities as a tank transporter prime mover, the same chassis has been chosen as the carrier for the British Army's new BR90 bridging system.

available in the RE4-P 4x4 chassis. Top hampers are built on the Unipower chassis by several well-known manufacturers; Carmichael of Worcester are the main partners for the UK market, but other companies include Angloco in Britain, Sides in France and Rosenbauer in Austria.

The latest Unipower range, and the first to be non-Scammell based, is the M Series forward-control 8x8 military vehicle, which can be used as a tank transporter, heavy recovery vehicle, DROPS self-loading truck or bridging system (BR90), as well as general cargo carrier and tanker. The engine, a 19-litre turbocharged and intercooled Cummins KTA-700 developing more than 700 bhp, is mounted behind the cab and drives through an automatic transmission. One of the lessons of the Gulf War was that double crewing was of great value, hence the large six-man cab of the M Series. This cab is made by Unipower, in contrast to those of other models which are by Motor Panels. Nine M Series Heavy Equipment Transporters have been supplied to the Royal Oman Army. These can carry a Challenger 2 Main Battle Tank or two Armoured Personnel Carriers. In contrast to the 8x8 M Series for the British Army, the Omani tractors have 6x6 drive.

In February 1994 the Unipower Group was acquired by defence equipment specialist (and former car maker) Alvis PLC for an initial consideration of £2 million. This expanded Alvis' activities in the defence industry, and gave Unipower greater manufacturing capability. It was fortunate as three months earlier Unipower had secured a £22.5 million contract to supply the vehicular element of the new BR90 bridging system for the Ministry of Defence. The BR90 vehicles are made in the Alvis works, while the M Series tank transporters are made at Watford. By October 1995 forty-five M Series BR90 units had been delivered for completion of bridging equipment.

Sad to say, the Tolpits Lane factory is no more. The buildings were let to various firms on temporary leases, the last of which expired in March 1994. The freehold was sold by Watford Council to Fairview Homes, who also acquired the Rover Group's long leasehold interest, and by October 1994 the site had been cleared so that work could start on building homes. These are a mix of studios, flats and houses and Fairview expect completion of more than 470 units by 1998. But if the factory and name of Scammell are gone, the tradition of purpose-built vehicles of high quality is continued by Unipower. Let us hope that Watford will be synonymous with such traditions for many years to come.

Above: An S26 6x4 aircraft refueller photographed at RAF Manston, Kent in the early 1990's. This example is equipped with refuelling booms. Running on low profile tyres, these refuellers, with slight modification, are capable of being conveyed in the RAF's C130 Lockheed Hercules transport aircraft.

Opposite page – top right and middle right: Scammell S26 models, serving with the RAF supporting its Mobile Radar system, photographed in the late 80's at RAF Coltishall, which was the engineering MT base for these vehicles. It could be argued that for the weight of the loads they had to tow or haul, they were somewhat over specified for the task.

Right: Prototype Scammell S26 6x6 heavy recovery vehicle. It was powered by a Rolls Royce E290L turbocharged engine coupled to a Fuller RTX 11609B, 8-speed gearbox and equipped with two main booms - one slewing and one towing.

Left: The AWD Multidrive was an ingenious system for giving an artic improved traction on loose or muddy surfaces, by powering the two axles of the semi-trailer. It was developed by a subsidiary of David J. Brown's dump truck business in Peterlee, County Durham, and applied to AWD, Scammell and Volvo FL10 motive units. The first S26 Multidrive was made in 1986, but few were built; because of the uncertainties at Watford, operators preferred to buy Volvo-based models.

Opposite right: This S26 heavy haulage tractor of Leicester Heavy Haulage, rated for 150 tonnes, began its working life with Pickfords. The load on the 4 and 6 axle King trailer equipped with a single axle jeep dolly is a 70 tonne Liebherr 974 excavator in the process of being moved in August 1990 from Bolventor, Nr Bodmin to Hatfield, Herts.

Left: Loyalty for the quality of the Watford product was deep founded. Knowles Transport of Wimblington, Cambs. bought five of these Roadtrain twin-steer tractors in the 1980s but insisted that they came complete with Scammell badging. This was changed at the local Leyland dealer; Ford & Slater of Peterborough. This example, pictured at Poole Docks, Dorset, left their fleet in 1987 having worked with its tri-axle trailer on agricultural haulage moving such commodities as bulk grain, animal feeds and sugar beet. Knowles current fleet is 75 strong, all being 38 tonne artics with Volvo or Scania tractor units.

Opposite right: A Scammell S26-fronted B-train running in the colours of NZL Transport on contract to Coastal Bottles Ltd., but owned by C.G. & L.A. Gray of Papamoa. The current maximum length these vehicles can currently operate at is 20 metres; their gross combination weight being 44 tonnes. Other examples of the S26 6x4 motive unit can be found working in New Zealand's highway logging industry and on refrigerated transport work. The country's trucks are fitted with hubometers which record kilometres travelled, the vehicle's operator purchasing kilometres in advance from the Department of Transport under its Road User Tax Scheme.

Left: Taunton Trucks operate this S26 heavy recovery unit from their Priorswood, Taunton facilities. It was acquired in 1992 by the company who modified and extended it to replace the AEC which previously fulfilled the role, its Dial Holmes 750 recovery equipment being transferred from that vehicle. Equipped with airbags, the ballasted unit operates under STO3 conditions having a maximum train weight rating of 100 tonnes. Power is provided to its Soma rear axles by a turbocharged Cummins NTE 350, uprated to 400 bhp, and 15-speed Fuller gearbox with deep reduction bottom gears. The Scammell dates originally from May 1986 and first operated as a medium-weight tractor with Tony Morgan Ltd of Bridgend.

Left: The Scammell S26 6x6 tractor formed the basis of this purposeful vehicle entered by Leyland France in the 1984 Paris-Dakar Rally. Over the years, this gruelling 6800 mile long event, which takes place at the beginning of each year commencing in France but subsequently traversing some of North Africa's hardest terrain before ending some twenty-one days later in the Senegalese capital, has sadly claimed the lives of a number of competitors including those competing in the truck categories. Fortunately the protective roll-over frame of this vehicle was not put to the test, however it did provide a more prominent place from where its true identity could be displayed

Left: A diesel multiple unit being transferred by road to Leicester for refurbishment by Vic Berry using a 4-axle King extendible trailer. This unusual S26 tractor, which began life with Derek Parnaby of County Durham, later passed into the fleet of Allelys Heavy Haulage who removed the front extension and refitted the standard S26 grille.

Below: Bristol-based Kings Heavy Haulage purchased three Scammell S26 6x4 tractor units in 1987, they being part of a cancelled export order. E630 NFB featured Leyland badging and was rated for 100 tonnes GTW although the load pictured here weighed only 20 tonnes. The ship's gun turret was in the process of being moved from the Dockyard at Devonport on a 55 tonne capacity Nooteboom tri axle trailer to an on-shore gunnery range at HMS Cambridge, Wembridge, South Devon during August 1992. This particular vehicle is no longer in service although its two stable mates still feature in the Kings fleet.

Right: A.L.E.'s Scammell S26 is usually used for hauling timber, girders, stands and equipment for the company's 'heavy gang', but on this occasion it was used for the hauling of a 58 ton fabrication from Barrow to Ardesier on a hired Interlift trailer. The location is Johnstonebridge on the A74 in October 1991.

Middle right: Scammell S26 6x4 tractor unit B135 MVT in Wynns/United Heavy Haulage livery. Seen here in articulated mode, the vehicle also works as a ballasted tractor, being equipped with a removable 20 tonne ballast box; power comes from a Cummins NTE 350 326 bhp engine. The high roof sleeper cab and extended side panels were modifications undertaken by Lancashire-based Cartwrights. The transformer load is being carried on a French-built Nicolas modular trailer.

Below: Photographed 'double heading' into the village of Roche, Cornwall during December 1995 were this duo of Econofreight operated Scammell S26 6x4 ballasted tractors. Grossing 190 tonnes, the combination were hauling an electrical transformer on an eight-axle Nicolas modular trailer from Portishead, Bristol to Fraddon. The lead unit, F300 PHN 'Evening Star' was the last heavy haulage tractor to leave the Watford factory. Its accompanying stablemate is 'Prince Harry', ex Wynns/United Heavy Transport. The name 'Evening Star' was the winning entry in a Commercial Motor competition. Other suggestions included 'King Harold' and 'The Colossus of Roads', the latter name being originally given to roadmaking pioneer Thomas Telford.

Above: A 1993 SNM6-D with the latest Carmichael cab, in service at Glasgow Airport. The 'D' or 'P' suffix does not indicate diesel or petrol (all are diesels), but denotes whether the vehicle is fitted with a power divider or PTO.

Opposite top: A Unipower built S24 oilfield vehicle with equipment by Halliburton, prior to being loaded onboard a ship destined for North Africa. The pumper unit is used for lining bore holes with cement. The link with Halliburton is long-lasting, as evidenced by the Constructor fire engine, illustrated on page 125, supplied thirty-six years earlier.

Left: An RAF Unipower Nubian 4x4 Mk10D, also of Carmichael origin, seen at RAF Scampton in the late 1980s. Note the extending light tower and the squared off engine compartment, other Mk10 models having a more rounded rear end.

Left: 1991-model RE6-P 6x6 crash tender with Carmichael top hamper in service at Southampton Airport. Unipower crash tenders and their Nubian predecessors are used at other British Airports including Heathrow, Birmingham, Cardiff, Glasgow and Guernsey, several British Aerospace airfields, and with the Royal Navy and Royal Air Force. The British Airports Authority has standardised on Unipower tenders for their major appliance replacement programme. Abroad they are in operation in 35 countries, including Tanzania, Ghana, Malaysia, New Zealand and the West Indies.

Opposite: An M Series 8x8 with DROPS self-loading equipment. The same chassis with bridging equipment is known as the BR90 (Bridging for the 90s), and it is also made for use with a tank transporter trailer.

Above and left: A study of old and new – a Unipower 'C' series 6x6 tractor unit alongside Econofreight's Mk 2 Scammell Contractor RWO 73R. The tractor was providing assistance (left), on steeper inclines to the movement of a 249 tonne high pressure column from the Air Products factory at Acrefair, North Wales to Ellesmere Port in February 1996, the company's S26 F300 PHN being the pusher vehicle at the rear of the load. The Unipower, rated for 240 tonnes GTW, is powered by a 14 litre Cummins 465 engine with a 16-speed ZF gearbox and ZF WSK400 torque converter. It has since received a pleasing high roofed crew cab conversion *(see page 182)* in Econofreight's Middlesborough workshops and now appears resplendent in the company's latest deep blue and white livery displaying their new corporate identity.

Left: One of a batch of Unipower M Series-based 6x6 Heavy Equipment Transporters that were waiting at Southampton Docks to be loaded onto a ship bound for Abu Dhabi, for eventual service with the Royal Omani Army. Power is provided by a turbocharged and intercooled 19-litre Cummins KTA-700 developing over 700 bhp, this being located behind the spacious six-man cab which itself is Unipower built. The unit is capable of transporting a Challenger 2 main battle tank or two armoured fighting vehicles.

CHAPTER TWELVE

Scammell in Colour

Above: A ballasted motive unit shudders its way slowly along the blockpaved Liverpool dock road in July 1967. In the background is British Railways' Langton Dock Goods Yard, Bootle. This early Fifties outfit with its unusual twin-oscillating axle type trailer loaded with steel joists, belonged to David Rees & Co. Ltd who ran a fleet of about fifteen lorries based at the Strand, Liverpool.

Left: This 'Showtrac', belonging to Webb's Amusements was photographed during the setting up of the summer fair at Luton's Manor Road site in June 1968. Only eighteen examples were built, this one dating from 1946 was delivered originally without Brown bodywork. The vehicle was first owned by John Flanagan passing to his niece, Alice Webb, on his death.

Above left: The ex military Pioneer of R. Edwards & Sons had the traditional 'coffee-pot', Scammell drive-line of a Gardner 6LW, gate-change gearbox and single differential giving chain and sprocket drive to the rear axles. It is pictured here, with rather poor paintwork in the days before they became particular with their livery, in the car park of the Swindon Town football stadium in 1970.

Above right: This Pioneer found a second life as a recovery vehicle with Chalker Commercials of Weymouth. This view dates from 1972 when the vehicle was photographed on the forecourt of the company's premises on the town's Granby Industrial Estate.

Left: A Scammell Explorer and Crusader owned by Ken Wills, of Cornwall Commercials enjoying a new lease of life at Brighton Cross Garage, Truro in 1991 as recovery vehicles. The Explorer, a 1955 model powered by a Leyland O.680 engine, was purchased from Ruddington in 1974 and in its civilian guise has pulled 70 tons, this being a transformer on a low loader. The Crusader, now a 6x4 and fitted with a Rolls Royce 290 engine, was previously a 4x2 tractor unit prior to acquiring the back tandem axle from a Leyland; its recovery equipment being self-built. The Explorer remains in service at the garage as at January 1997.

Above: The Scammell Showtrac 'Gladiator' is the longest working example existing, supplied new to George De Vey in April 1946, it worked with Anderton & Rowland's No.2 Section right up to 1995. It is seen here pulling onto Plympton Fairground during the summer of 1981 towing the Dodgem power unit and living accommodation.

Opposite left: In the post-war years much military hardware found a second life in the civilian world. Siddle C Cook's Scammell Mountaineer 200 APT is seen here with a large fabrication carried on two ex-military tank transporter trailers.

Right: Taken in February 1966, this photograph shows a British Railways Scarab in BR (Midlands) livery, coupled to a Rail Freight van trailer. It was captured on film in Park Street, Luton and was based at the town's Midland Road Goods Depot.

Above: Scammell's Routeman 1 was a short-lived model bridging the brief period between the end of 'Rigid Eight' production in 1959 and the launch of the futuristic 'Michelotti' cabbed Routeman 2 in 1962. The United Molasses Co. of Liverpool was noted for their smart fleet of Scammell tankers.

Left: A classic example of Scammell's distinctive 'Michelotti' cabbed Routeman 3 8x4 tipper with tipping body for gravel and aggregates. It was one of a fleet operated by Kidwelly based I.T. Thomas in Dyfed, South Wales and was brand new when photographed in April 1976.

Top right: Still going strong in the late Sixties, this Rigid Eight belies its early wartime origins. Registered in 1940 it was one of a large fleet amassed by Syd Harrison of Sheffield following denationalisation in 1953. Most were completely refurbished by having new cabs and Gardner 150 engines later in life. Loaded with motor component stillages for Ford's factory, the lorry is seen heading around the North Circular Road in London in September 1968.

Middle right: This Routeman bulk-blower of Amey Roadstone would occasionally carry powdered stone to France and Germany, hence the TIR plates and additional driving lamps. It was photographed at their Chipping Sodbury depot in 1977.

Bottom right: The Cement Marketing Company operated a very large fleet of Routeman eight wheelers with a mixture of bulk tank and flat bodies. This 1974 example was photographed in 1978.

Left: Lea Valley Dairies, Burr Street bottling plant at Luton is the setting for this January 1970 view of a 1946 'Artic Eight' motive unit which is shod on 40x8 wheels and tyres. It was unusual to see a 'solo' motive unit, since Scammell 'Artic Eights' were designed as 'permanently coupled' vehicles, employing Scammell's own unique 'Spherub' ball-and-socket coupling.

Below, bottom left and right: Wynn's Highwayman WDW 383, fleet no. 179, entered service with the company in 1960. It is seen here surmounting a rise on the A4 adjacent to the 'Ridgeway' Transport Cafe in the pre-M4 Motorway days of 1970. It is heading home with a relatively modest load probably secured to cover the cost of the diesel although the fact that it carries a crew implies that the outward journey consisted of a load something more substantial. The location was a favourite haunt of photographer Adrian Cypher who also captured on film this tidy looking Highwayman, operated by Miller and Gordon of Liverpool & London, with its load of electric cabling. Earlier, in 1967, he photographed this two year old 'Handyman' with step-frame trailer, rated to operate at 24 ton GCW. Owned by J. Dyke, haulage contractors based at Chelmsford, Essex, the relatively new vehicle was already showing signs of wear and tear.

Above: This 1961 registered Highwayman features the old style Scammell front axle, and, at first sight, looks every inch the traditional 'Artic Eight'. However, it features a standard fifth wheel coupling and wind-down trailer support legs. The operator was the London Co-operative Society and the photograph was taken at the Thatcham MMB depot in June 1969.

Right: The bonnetted Highwayman tractor was synonymous with Leonard J. Stamp's fleet during that haulage operator's formative years. However, MHW 492F was ten years old when this picture was taken in their Avonmouth yard in 1977 and their allegiance to the type had long given way to examples of Scammell's Handyman 4 model, although these were still Gardner powered. By this time the company had been acquired by the United Transport group but was still retaining its original identity.

Right: The growing need for larger trailers in the early Sixties led Scammell to break with tradition and produce a 'cabover' version of their motive unit. It was dubbed the 'Handyman' and featured a fibreglass cab. This one was based at Rotherham and is seen unloading sheet steel at a large motor factory in October 1970. Later models were to feature the Michelotti cab as fitted to Scammell's Trunker and Routeman models.

Left: Although its well-used appearance gives some indication of the hard work that it was subject to, this Scammell Trunker, EAR 740F, seen here in the owners yard in Lydiard Millicent in 1973, was in fact quite an interesting vehicle. It was purchased secondhand, having started life as a demonstrator in the fleet of Scammell Lorries. Its special feature was a pneumo-cyclic semi-automatic gearbox, giving two pedal control. It proved very satisfactory in service and prompts one to wonder why it was never made a standard fitting.

Opposite right: Scammell Sales Director Peter Redfern's proposal to NFC's Walter Batstone of a 6x4 Crusader cut down to a 4x2 with a 220 bhp Rolls Royce diesel and Leyland heavy rear axle eventually resulted in the model being adopted as British Road Services' standard long distance trunk vehicle for the new Seventies era. This brand new example was captured on film by Peter Davies at Great Shelford near Cambridge in June 1972.

Left: This unusual 1973 Scammell Trunker sleeper-cabbed tractor had just returned from a long haul to Portugal when photographed during 1983. Powered by a Rolls Royce 265L engine, the ex Ross Foods vehicle was operated by Wiltshire-based owner/driver Norman Howard.

Below: This Crusader 6x4 powered by a Detroit 8V71 two-stroke, is operated by Oregon Hauling Co. who run a fleet of logging trucks on New Zealand's North Island. Stan Williamson, the owner of the company, bought the last Crusaders imported into the country, acquiring 12 examples in March 1983, ten years prior to when this photograph was taken at the weighbridge at Rainbow Mountain.

Right: Rumours of gross weight increases in the early Seventies led many U.K. manufacturers and operators to experiment with bigger artics at 40 to 44 tonnes design weight. This monster five axle outfit was undergoing trials with Bass Charrington Breweries and was photographed at the group's Mitchells & Butlers Cape Hill brewery in Birmingham in April 1971. The tractor unit is a 6x4 Crusader featuring the newly adopted Motor Panels Mk3 cab. Note the wide spread (20 tonne) trailer bogie on super single tyres.

Above: Nearing the end of its working life with the Royal Corp of Logistics, this Leyland badged Crusader with an appropriate load was pictured on the square of the 19th Tank Transporter Squadron, Bulford Camp, Wiltshire in September 1995. The Squadron's Crusaders were due to be replaced by new Seddon Atkinson units, the first of which was scheduled to be delivered that coming November.

Left: The Crusader was a conventional motive unit with non-tilting steel cab made by Motor Panels, and Rolls-Royce Eagle engines in normally-aspirated and turbo-charged models. Standard gearbox was a 15-speed Fuller Roadranger. British Road Services acquired many examples of the type and other operators introduced the model into their fleets. The example illustrated here being in the livery of Chris Bennett Heavy Haulage of Wilmslow, Cheshire.

Left: This Crusader was one of a number to join the fleet of Bailey's of Westbury Ltd. as a result of their takeover of the Heron Group Truck Rental fleet. The vehicle was fitted out for Middle East work with additional storage lockers and air-conditioning. Powered by a blown Rolls-Royce Eagle 280 it is seen at Bailey's premises on the West Wilts Trading Estate in Westbury in 1981.

Above: This splendid scene was captured on film in 1973 by Adrian Cypher who, having absented himself from the office by way of a fictitious errand, scaled an adjacent water-tower in order to obtain the best possible vantage point for a photograph. The location is the Swindon works of British Rail Engineering Ltd and the preserved 4-4-2 tank locomotive, which had just had its running gear overhauled by BREL, is being winched aboard the Crane 100-ton girder frame trailer before being returned to its then current home by Sunter's Super Constructor.

Right: Sunters Junior Constructor 6x4 HPY 64D and Super Constructor 6x6 447 DPY with Crane girder frame trailers of 90 ton and 100 ton capacity respectively. In common with Pickfords, Sunters had removed the skirts from under the ballast boxes to save on maintenance and repairs. They were always being caught by obstructions in factories and works.

Left: This 150 ton GTW standard-cabbed Scammell Contractor was one of a number operated by the famous Wynns of Newport concern, joining their fleet in 1967. In this instance it appears to be working well within its limits with a 'two-bed-two' girder frame trailer. It was photographed at Toddington Motorway Services on the M1 in September 1969.

Right: A crew-cabbed Contractor of A.L.E. pictured at Leigh Delamere Services in 1995. This vehicle used to work in Finland, hence the Q-prefixed registration number. The company had been engaged in a considerable number of movements of heavy components from Avonmouth Docks, Bristol to Didcot, Oxfordshire and the location was used as a staging point along the M4 corridor. In the background is one of the company's 6x6 Faun tractor units, the main prime movers utilised for the task.

Left: One of two 6x4 Contractors imported from Norway by A.L.E. - the other having caught fire in Holland whilst in transit, it being subsequently cannibalised to keep this example running. The picture dates from 1991 when the vehicle was used in the construction of the A38 Marsh Mills flyover in Plymouth, the load comprising of a 200ft steel bridge beam weighing 110 tonnes on 6 & 8 row Nicolas modular bogies. This Contractor lasted until 1996 when it was also scrapped for spares.

Above: An impressive study of Sunter's first 240 tonne Contractor TPY 675H which entered service with the company in June 1970. It is pictured here with a six-axle Crane girder trailer loaded with ship fabrications by Whessoe of Darlington. It was later rebuilt and re-registered as YVN 308T, an illustration of which appears on page 175. It now serves with Lift and Shift of India, who feature elsewhere in this book, having been exported to them in the mid 1980s.

Right: Martin Phippard's impressive early morning study of Pointer's 240-ton Contractor MVG 90H parked up behind Southampton's swimming baths in the early 1970s, having delivered a load on its Dyson trailer into the nearby docks the previous day. The Contractor later passed into the fleet of northern heavy haulage operator Kaye Goodfellow before being exported to Saudi Arabia.

Above: A 320 ton transformer built by N.E.I. Peebles at Edinburgh being transported on 18th August 1988 to Leith Docks carried on Nicolas 12ft wide trailers and hauled by Econofreight's Stafford-based Mk 2 Contractors 'Challenger' and 'Superior'. The outfit is seen here climbing the 1:6 bank at Silver Knowse.

Below: The heavy tractors of A.L.E. have recently been a familiar sight along the M4 corridor with their abnormal loads of heavy electrical equipment being conveyed between the Avonmouth Docks and the Didcot B Power Station. However, an equally impressive movement took place in Cornwall in March 1996 when the company moved a 220 tonne stator generator between Penzance and the Indian Queens sub-station. It is seen here on the A30 Redruth by-pass and company Scammells - 240 ton Contractor and S24 'Trident' - are heading up the load which is mounted on a Cometto frame trailer equipped with Nicolas modular bogies. Assistance at the rear being is provided by one of their 6x6 Faun prime movers.

Opposite right: Evolution in more ways than one - 240-ton Contractors in ITM-Sunter and United Heavy Transport liveries alongside Wynns Mk 2 Contractor 'Invincible'. Sunters YVN 802T began life as TPY 675H, being subsequently rebuilt and re-registered. All three liveries were later to give way to the blue and white of Econofreight.

Above: Pickfords two Mk 2 Contractors cause traffic consternation as they haul 344 tons of generator inner core on board the Nicolas girder frames, and the company's Volvo F12 tractor on its first day out, up the 1:6 hill into Gateshead en route from Birtley to the Albert Edward dock on North Tyneside. Photographer Keith Nicholl recalls the unforgettable bellow of the Cummins' reverberating between the adjacent houses.

Overleaf: A 152 tonne Hawker-Siddeley transformer being moved from Teignmouth Docks to Alverdiscott near Torrington, North Devon on 22nd October 1983. The location is the A30 between Exeter & Torrington. The leading Wynns Scammell 240 ton Mk 2 Contractor is DBF 134Y 'Revenge' – the last crew-cabbed Contractor built. Bringing up the rear are Mk 2s DBO 661V 'Invincible' and RWO 73R 'Superior' – the second and first Mk 2 examples respectively, purchased by Wynns. The load grossed 350 tonnes and the transformer was carried on a 12-axle Crane girder trailer fitted with air-cushion blowing equipment for use when crossing weak bridges along the route.

Above: This resplendent Commander, seen here at Bulford with its Crane Fruehauf trailer in September 1995, had recently arrived back with the 19th Tank Transporter Squadron after undergoing a total rebuild and refurbishment by Unipower. It had last seen service in Saudi Arabia with the Allied forces in the 1991 Gulf War during which time it suffered accidental fire damage, being almost gutted.

Left: The Essex Fire Service Scammell S24 6x6 heavy purpose recovery unit was acquired by Somerset Rescue of Biddisham, Somerset in June 1996 and is pictured here at the company's premises resplendent in its new livery and fitted with mud-terrain tyres. Power is provided by a turbo aftercooled Cummins NTE 350 coupled to an Allison 5-speed automatic gearbox and the unit is equipped with a Concept 3000 recovery unit by Boniface Engineering; two H30 winches and airbags are also part of the equipment specification. The chassis is understood to be one of only two examples of the type built, the other being exported to Malaysia where it worked as a tipper on the construction of the Punwar Dam.

Right: This Econofreight Scammell S24, rated for 150 tons GTW, was originally equipped as a ballast box tractor but was later refitted as an artic unit. It is seen here on 15th August 1992 with a skid frame for the unloading of oil rig modules from barges made by PIAM Engineering of Workington and loaded on an ex-Wynns Nicolas trailer.

Left: Like its Scammell predecessors, the S24 serves as a platform for a great many tasks. This 6x4 example is equipped with a Relex 115W all purpose hydraulically operated exploratory and water well drilling rig manufactured by Ritchies Equipment of Dunblane, Perthshire. It is capable of drilling to depths in excess of 400 metres; a Ford 2726 T industrial diesel providing the necessary auxiliary power.

Right: This impressive S26 6x4 outfit running at 32 ton GTW went into service with Cuprinol Products of Frome in 1981. The first of six similar vehicles that saw service with the company, it was powered by the 265L Rolls Royce engine feeding through a 10-speed Spicer gearbox. The fleet was used on hauling the company's products from its manufacturing plant to timber yards, DIY outlets and other trade facilities all over the U.K., the demountable boxes being interchangeable with tanks as necessary. The last vehicle was out of service by 1994, but two soldier on elsewhere having been converted to wreckers.

Above: Halls of Christchurch Scammell S26 -fronted 'B' train, was a long way from home when this picture was taken in Wellington, New Zealand, having travelled up some 500 miles from its base in the country's South Island, a journey that also necessitates crossing the 60-mile wide Cook Strait that separates the country's two main islands. Halls also employ Scania and Seddon Atkinson motive power units in their refrigerated transport fleet.

Left: S26 ballasted tractors of the RAF's Mobile Radar System photographed at RAF Coltishall in the late 1980s. Other S26 models in service with the unit include 6x4s for operation as articulated tractors.

Left: The last truck to be made at Tolpits Lane, chassis No. J72969, was laid down on 25th May 1988. It was ordered by Swansea Truck Centre for their customers, Westland Coal Suppliers Ltd of Newport. The customer insisted it was badged as a Scammell, though most Constructor 8s carried Leyland Badges.

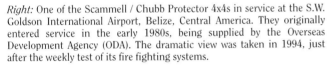

Above and below: Scammell Nubian Major 6x6 / Gloster-Saro crash trucks of the RAF Fire & Rescue Service. The Mk11A below is one of two based at Mount Pleasant Airport, Falklands Islands, South Atlantic. The RAF operates both Mk11 and Mk11A trucks, the latter carrying an elevating 10 metre platform. Capacity of the Mk11A is 1250 gallons water; 150 gallons foam. The vehicle is seen undergoing its weekly test, on this occasion only water being used. The photograph dates from 1987 and was taken by Alan Godfree, he verified it was a very cold and snowy winter on the Falklands that year! The other view is of a Mk11 model, based in the U.K. and finished in the more traditional red livery.

Right: One of the Scammell / Chubb Protector 4x4s in service at the S.W. Goldson International Airport, Belize, Central America. They originally entered service in the early 1980s, being supplied by the Overseas Development Agency (ODA). The dramatic view was taken in 1994, just after the weekly test of its fire fighting systems.

Above: Impressive is the only way to describe this action photo of a Unipower M Series-based Heavy Equipment Transporter of the Army of Oman transporting one of its eighteen Vickers Defence Systems 62.5 tonne Challenger MkII main battle tanks. Nine of these Cummins KTA-700 6x6 transporters capable of 85 kph fully laden, equipped with a six-man crew cab and fully-steered multi-axle trailer, are in service with that Army.

Right: M Series 8x8 production-standard prototypes on test near Aldershot with the Royal Engineers. Powered by Euro-2 Perkins 410Tx feeding through a ZF Ecomat 6HP 900 fully automatic transmission, these mighty transporters have revealed truly outstanding cross-country capabilities. The first production batch of 20 has now entered service with a further 119 to follow.

Right: Econofreight's Unipower 'C' type heavy duty tractor unit N523 YAJ in the company's new livery at their Middlesborough depot in the Autumn of 1996. It had just emerged from their workshops where it had received the crew cab conversion, it blending in well with the vehicles functional lines.

Scammell Chassis Numbers 1922 – 1988

1922 - 1967

The chassis numbering system, introduced in 1922 by the original company, started at 700. Whether this was due to the use of the 7-litre engine or because of the 7-7½ ton payload capability - according to the weight of the body fitted to the carrier - is now lost in the mists of time.

By the time that the Scammell 100 Tonners were built in 1929, chassis number 1429 had been reached. However, then came the depression, and by the end of the 1930s the chassis numbers of the heavy vehicles had still only reached the 2000 mark. The Mechanical Horses were numbered in a separate series.

During World War II production expanded considerably, these mostly being 6x4 Pioneers in the heavy range, although limited numbers of civilian vehicles were produced for essential transport needs, and by 1945 chassis numbers had reached 5000.

The Showtracs of 1946 were numbered in the 6000 series and numbers continued to climb through the 1950s reaching the 10000 point around 1960. During 1962 at chassis number 10550 there came a change of policy. The chassis numbers were 'jumped' to catch up with the sales orders. Previously the gap between these had grown steadily due to the sales of carriers (trailers) only, and also in the earlier days because of refurbishing work carried out both for customers and on vehicles taken in part exchange.

Next came a period when the chassis number (from about 13500 onwards) was common to the sales order. This lasted until 1st October 1967 when, along with the rest of the Leyland Group, Scammell adopted the three alpha prefix and a new series of numbers. It is difficult to pin point the last of the old system numbers as the sales orders were not built in strict rotation. Take the Highwayman for example - of the 47 allocated WHV numbers, the sales orders range from 19861 to 22344.

1967 - 1980/85

The new Leyland Group system allocated Scammell the following prefixes:

WHV for Watford Heavy Vehicle
WLV for Watford Light Vehicle
WHT for Watford Heavy Trailer
WLT for Watford Light Trailer

Other variations were:

BLVxxxxx – light vehicle built at Thornycroft, Basingstoke
BHVxxxxx – heavy vehicle built at Thornycroft, Basingstoke
BHVxxxxxW – allocated to Thornycroft, Basingstoke but completed at Scammell, Watford
DNxxxxx – Grantham built Aveling Barford or Barfords of Belton. LD55 only
GHVxxxxx – Scammell 4x2 Crusaders built at Guy Motors, Fallings Park, Wolverhampton.
WHVxxxxxB – allocated to Watford, but built by Thornycroft, Basingstoke.
WHVxxxxxMP – built at Moor Park, Scammell No.2 works.

Numerical Listing	First Chassis Laid	Last Chassis Laid
DN 099 to DN 539 LD55(AV690) Dump Truck	26.06.69	14.01.76
WHV 1001 to WHV 1047 Highwayman 4x2	04.10.67	11.02.70
WHV 2001 to WHV 2392 Routeman 2 8x2	22.11.67	09.02.72
Note: some with suffix B – subcontracted to Basingstoke.		
WHV 2701 to WHV 2999 Routeman 3 8x4	05.12.69	21.08.70
Note: some with suffix MP – built at Moor Park works, Watford.		
WHV 3001 to WHV 3169 Super Constructor	18.10.67	23.04.81
WHV 4001 to WHV 5208 Contractor 6x4 & Iraq Explorer 6x6	07.11.67	12.05.83
WHV 5001 to WHV 5011 Mountaineer 4x4	09.01.68	26.06.72
Note the overlap of numbers in above two series.		
BHV 6001 to BHV 6042 Sherpa 4x2 dumper	22.12.67	12.12.68
Note: some with suffix W - built at Watford.		
BLV 7001 to BLV ???? Townsman (last not known)	n/a	n/a
BHV 8001 to BHV 8020 Nubian Major 6x6 TFA/B81	07.02.68	05.06.70
BHV 9001 to BHV 9124 Nubian Major TMA 300 & V903	19.03.68	00.12.72
WHV 9125 to WHV 9443 Nubian Major V903 (Front Engine)	00.01.73	21.08.79
BHV 10001 to BHV 10355 LD 55	10.04.68	29.03.71
WHV 10400 to WHV 10731 LD 55 & LD 24 (LD55 Mk2-19 Vehicles)	04.02.75	19.12.80
WHV 11001 to WHV 11999 Trunker 6x2	03.10.67	29.10.70
WHV 12000 to WHV 12999 Handyman 4x2	11.10.67	25.06.70
BHV 13001 to BHV 13082 Himalayan 6x4	n/a	26.01.72
Note: all carry suffix W – built at Watford		
WHV 13083 to WHV 13111 Himalayan 6x4	22.09.72	22.03.75
WLV 14001 to WLV ????? Scarab (last not known)	n/a	n/a
WHV 52001 to WHV 52999 Crusader 6x4 & 4x2	28.08.68	04.06.74
WHV 53000 to WHV 53999 Crusader 6x4 & 4x2	04.06.74	16.02.79
Note: last Watford built 4x2 WHV 53238, remainder all 6x4		

WHV 54001 to WHV 54999 Handyman 4x2	25.03.70	06.03.74
WHV 55001 to WHV 55999 Routeman 3 8x4	21.08.70	19.03.73
WHV 56001 to WHV 56712 Trunker 6x2	30.10.70	14.08.73
WHV 57001 to WHV 57999 Routeman 3 8x4	19.03.73	05.12.74
WHV 58001 to WHV 58039 Handyman 4x2	06.03.74	20.06.74
GHV 59001 to GHV 59539 Crusader 4x2	11.02.75	00.00.81
WHV 60001 to WHV 61999 Routeman 8x4	05.12.74	08.11.79
WHV 62001 to WHV 62109 Rear Engine Crash Tender	18.04.77	10.05.85
WHV 63001 to WHV 63223 Crusader 6x4	06.12.77	24.11.81
WHV 65000 to WHV 65811 Marathon (Proprietary engines)	12.11.79	02.05.80
WHV 66000 to WHV 66261 Routeman 3 8x4	12.11.79	02.05.80

1980 – 1985

A new numbering system was introduced in 1980 to meet EEC regulations incorporating the year of build into the V.I.N. (Vehicle Identification Number), this being a prefix alpha letter, commencing with A for 1980. Exceptions to the new numbering system were the Nubian rear-engined crash tenders which, until 31st July 1985, continued to be numbered under the existing three alpha prefix system.

The first chassis number series to follow the three alpha prefix format was used on the Constructor 8 and derivatives only. Starting at A8T57P30000001 (laid down by experimental – date unknown).

The first known date is for chassis A8T57P30000006 laid down 28.2.80.
The series continued up to chassis A8T56P30000411 laid down 27.2.81.

Following the above series Scammell were allocated 70000 to 79999, which were sub-allocated by model type as follows:

70001 to 73999 Constructor 8 & derivatives.
74001 to 75999 S24

76001 to 77999 S26 and derivatives including T45 6x2 Roadtrain
78000 to 78499 Commander
78500 to 78999 T43 Scammell built only
79001 to 79999 S26 6x6 & 8x6 Military

This series continued until August 1985 when the integrated numbering system was introduced. The last chassis numbers allocated under the separate model system were:-

Constructor 8	G 71962 laid down	06.08.85
S24	F 74115 " "	04.07.85
S26 & T45 6x2	F 77037 " "	05.08.85
Commander	F 78124 " "	19.12.84
S26 Military	G 79125 " "	27.09.85

When Leyland Landtrain production was transferred back to Scammell after the closure of B.M.C. Bathgate, it was allocated the series beginning F 78500 laid down 26.5.85, reaching F 78570 by 5.8.85. After this it was incorporated in the new integrated system.

1985 – 1988

From August 1985 the integrated numbering system was introduced – irrespective of type - for all 'built up' chassis from the Scammell plant, commencing with G 70001. This re-use of existing chassis numbers revealed the importance of the prefix year letter, it being the only way to delineate between the new and existing series.

Chassis supplied in 'Knocked Down' (KD) kit form were allocated F 78500, the first being dated 26.5.85.

The last chassis built at Scammell's Tolpits Lane Works was J 72969. This was laid down on the 25th May 1988 and was a Constructor 8.

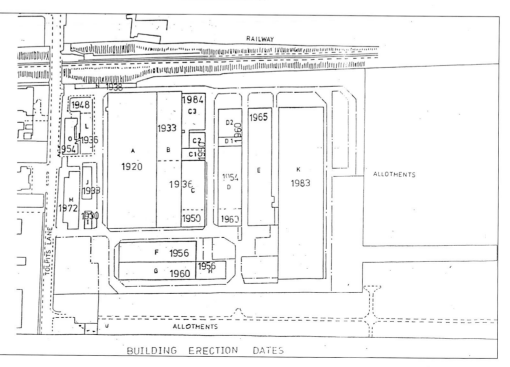

SCAMMELL MOTORS WATFORD PLANT

Site plan of Scammell Motors plant at Tolpits Lane, Watford, Hertfordshire as it existed in the mid 1980s. Although closure was just around the corner, significant new buildings were still being erected as late as 1984, the new assembly hall being funded from the sale of the Moor Park works, indicative of the lack of longer term strategic planning existing within the company's Leyland-based hierarchy. Note also the nearby allotments, these were to provide a familiar backdrop to many of the official photographs of Scammell vehicles over the years, especially many of the pre-war examples.